THE BOOK OF ADAM TO MOSES

THE BOOK
OF ADAM TO MOSES

Lore Segal and Leonard Baskin

ALFRED A. KNOPF · NEW YORK

Acknowledgments

I want to thank Deirdre Levinson and other
Hebrew-speaking friends of whom I kept inquiring
over the telephone. My thanks to Maier Deshell,
who helped me understand what must not be left
out; to Peter Schweitzer, who wouldn't let me get
away with anything; and, above all, to Rabbi Jules
Harlow for the long and patient afternoons when
he worked with me over this text.

— L. S.

Book design by Denise Cronin

10 9 8 7 6 5 4 3 2 1

Library of Congress Cataloging-in-Publication Data

Segal, Lore Groszmann. The book of Adam to Moses.

Summary: A Modern English version of the stories
of the five books of Moses.
1. Bible. O.T. Pentateuch—Paraphrases, English.
[1. Bible. O.T. Pentateuch—Paraphrases]
I. Baskin, Leonard, 1922–   , ill. II. Title.
BS1226.S44   1987   222'.105209   87–2581
ISBN 0-394-86757-2   ISBN 0-394-96757-7 (lib. bdg.)

CONTENTS

PREFACE

THERE ARE THOSE FOR WHOM the Bible is a God-given Book. Scholars suppose it to be a collection of oral and written traditions beginning three thousand years ago. If this archaic work survives into the twentieth century it is because it constitutes a basic strain in our thinking. That other grand strain, the Greek, has already slipped out of our general education; the Bible is slipping because, for good and sufficient reason, it is not part of the American curriculum.

The Bible is not a book only of religion, laws, lessons—of the answers antiquity gave to the ur-questions. The teachings come to us in the form of incomparable stories with characters who, like ourselves, act both familiarly and incomprehensibly. On the vast stage of the new-made world they are sometimes faithful and sometimes disobedient; they get hungry, they want children; have friendships; grieve when they are unloved; they work, despair, murder, go mad. The narrative mode is subtle, devious, double and triple. It is funny. The stories enter your life. It is no wonder the book's been two and a half thousand years on the best-seller list. How can we bear for our children to miss this?

New versions, retranslations for children, for the general reader, for the scholar, continue to proliferate in the bookstores. Why did we undertake to do yet another? The excuse is every translator's inexcusable arrogance: I can do it better.

We have told the part of the story contained in the first five of the thirty-nine books of the Hebrew Bible, which Christendom calls the Old Testament. And these are the stories the Koran tells to Islam. Most of the narrative is found in Genesis and Exodus, but we have had no qualms—or, to speak the truth, had a lot of qualms—helping ourselves to portions of the other Five Books of Moses. We have been at pains not to retell what tells itself so wonderfully well. We did not want to introduce the sort of detail we have learned to expect from modern realistic fiction, nor to simplify, nor explain, nor add or alter anything except for the alteration inherent in leaving out. We have included the Ten Commandments but not the great body of laws that instructs the children of Israel how to build their altars and dress their sacrifices and teach us human conscience and compassion. And we have sacrificed some of the repetition that constitutes the Bible's natural mode because it seems to be a roadblock to the modern reader. We mean the reader to run, afterward, and read the whole Bible.

In the third century B.C.E. the Torah was translated into the Greek version called the Septuagint, meaning seventy. Legend says that seventy-two scholars sat in seventy-two cells and came out on the seventy-second day with seventy-two identical translations of the sacred text.

We are not so blessed. My method was to compare old and new English and German versions, taking advantage of the sophisticated modern scholarship of *The Torah*, *A Modern Commentary*, as well as the poetry of the seventeenth-century King James Bible, translated by a convocation of scholars who had the language of Shakespeare at their service. One of my two German sources was Luther's magnificent sixteenth-century translation; it is said to have changed the German language. The other was the beautiful translations Martin Buber and Franz Rosenzweig began in the first decades of our century by returning to the original Hebrew.

Howard Nemerov has defined poetry as "getting something right in language." Translation wants to take something that is right in one language and get it right in another. This translator wanted to perfectly render the ancient texts into perfect current English that feels inevitable, sans antique or antic vocabulary, without forced or fancy-dress syntax. Translators are like children on New Year's Day: *This* time we will be perfect. But before we reach the end of the second sentence we remember—there are no synonyms; no word precisely overlaps any other. An edge of meaning has got lost, a shade not in the original has accrued. Or if the meaning is exact, there's a missing resonance or an unwanted pun, a smidgen too much or too little weight, the wallop of slang the original doesn't recognize. Or we've got one syllable too many! The rhythm is ruined!

What is more, our Bible speaks out of a world of which we are mainly ignorant. When childless Sarah offers her slave girl as surrogate mother to bear Abraham a child, might we sneak it into the text that it was the custom? No. We may not sneak. And we have made a covenant with ourselves to leave the mysteries alone: Do two or three men or angels visit Abraham in his tent?

And there are words that denote experience we do not have. When Rebekah "enquired of the Lord" why the twins struggled in her womb, she engaged in a dialogue of a sort the heavens no longer vouchsafe us. She can't be translated to be praying to the Lord nor asking nor consulting, questioning, interrogating, pumping, or sounding Him out. No thesaurus will find us the right verb for an activity of which we have no exact concept. Why not just put that she "enquired"? Because Modern English does not let us say so.

Or, how do we translate the word the King James text renders as "behold," Luther as *siehe*? Some moderns translate "look." "Look" will do—though we are more likely to say "listen" when one human wants another to pay attention. But "look" does not *feel* right when it occurs in a dialogue between God and man, in either direction: Why not leave it out, then, since it adds nothing to content? Because we would lose a looseness in the rhythm, the sense of presence, of connectedness between the divine and the human having a conversation.

And so one broods over each recurrence of each problem and keeps trying it this way and that, unable, ever, entirely, to abandon hope of, sooner or later, getting it exactly right.

And finally, I have retained the "and . . . and" construction though it may irritate the modern ear, which expects to hear "when . . . then." A footnote in Robert Alter's *The Art of Biblical Narrative* explains to me my own instinct in this matter: statements connected by "and" have equal value, whereas clauses beginning with "whereas," "when," "because," "although" not only subordinate one to another but specify their logical relationship in a way the Bible generally does not. Why should we be wiser?

— *Lore Segal*

THE BOOK OF ADAM TO MOSES

In the beginning God created the heavens and the earth. The earth was without form, and empty, and the breath of God moved over the face of the waters.

God said, Let there be light, and there was light. And God saw that the light was good. And God divided the light from the darkness.

God called the light Day, and the darkness He called Night. There was evening and there was morning, the first day.

God said, Let there be a firmament between the waters, and let it divide the waters.

And God made the firmament, and divided the waters under the firmament from the waters over the firmament, and it was so.

God called the firmament Heaven. And there was evening and there was morning, the second day.

God said, Let the waters under the heavens come together in one place and let dry land appear, and it was so.

God called the dry land Earth and the

coming together of the waters He called Seas, and God saw that it was good.

God said, Let the earth bear plants that have seeds, and trees that grow fruit that have seeds, each of its own kind, and it was so. The earth bore plants that had seeds, each of its own kind, and trees that grew fruit that had seeds of its own kind. And God saw that it was good.

And there was evening and there was morning, the third day.

God said, Let there be lights in the heavens to divide the day from the night, and distinguish the seasons, and mark the days and years, and let the lights shine upon the earth. And it was so.

And God made two great lights, the greater light to rule over the day, and the lesser light to rule over the night. He made the stars and set them in the heavens to shine upon the earth. And God saw that it was good.

And there was evening and there was morning, the fourth day.

God said, Let the waters swarm with living things, and let birds fly on the earth under the heavens. And God created the great monsters of the sea and every living and every creeping thing that swarms in the waters, each of its own kind, and every winged bird of its own kind. And God saw that it was good.

God blessed them and said, Be fruitful, multiply and fill the waters of the sea, and let the birds multiply on the earth.

And there was evening and there was morning, the fifth day.

And God said, Let the earth bear living creatures. And it was so. God made wild animals of every kind, and cattle of every kind, and every kind of creeping thing, each of its own kind. And God saw that it was good.

And God said, Let Us make man in Our image, in Our own likeness, and let them rule over the fish of the sea and the birds of the heavens, and over the cattle on the earth and over the wild animals and over every thing that creeps on the ground.

So God created man in His own image, in the likeness of God He created him, male and female He created them.

And God blessed them and God said, Be fruitful and multiply and fill the earth and rule over it. Rule over the fish of the sea and over the birds in the air and over every living thing that moves on the earth.

God said, Look! I give you every plant that grows on the earth, and every tree that bears fruit. They shall be your food. To every beast of the earth and every bird in the air, and to every thing that creeps on the earth and breathes with life, I have given the green plants for food. And it was so.

And God saw everything that He had made, and yes, it was very good!

And there was evening and there was morning, the sixth day.

And so the heavens were finished, and the earth, and all the things that are on it. On the seventh day God was finished with all the work that He had done, and everything that He had made. And God blessed the seventh day and made it holy, because it was the day on which He rested from all His work and all He had created and made.

That is how the heavens and the earth were created.

⁂

NOW ON THE DAY when the Lord God made the heavens and the earth, there was no shrub growing in the field and no plant sprouting out of the ground, because the Lord God had not yet made it rain on the earth, and there was no man to till the ground.

And a mist rose out of the ground and watered the fields, and the Lord God formed a man out of the dust of the field. Into his nostrils He blew the breath of life, and man became a living creature.

The Lord God planted a garden in Eden in the east and He took the man that He had made and put him in the garden

to till it and care for it. Out of the ground the Lord God brought forth every kind of tree that was beautiful and good to eat, and into the middle of the garden He put the tree of life and the tree of the knowledge of good and evil.

And the Lord God commanded the man and said, You may eat the fruit of every tree in the garden. Eat as much as you like, except for the fruit of the tree of the knowledge of good and evil, which you may not eat, for on the day you eat it, you will have to die.

And the Lord God said, It is not good for man to be alone. I shall make him a companion, to be with him.

And the Lord God made all the beasts on the earth and all the birds in the heavens and He brought them to Adam to see what he would call them, and whatever Adam called each living creature, that was its name. But for Adam there was no companion to be with him.

And the Lord God let a deep sleep fall upon Adam. Adam slept, and God took one of his ribs and closed up the place with his flesh, and out of the rib the Lord God formed a woman, and brought her to the man.

Adam said, This is she who is bone of my bone and flesh of my flesh. She shall be called wo-man because she was taken out of man. That is why a man leaves his father and his mother and becomes one flesh with his wife.

And Adam named the woman Eve, meaning Life Giver, and she became the mother of all who are alive.

And they were both naked, the man and his wife, and were not ashamed.

ʕ ʕ ʕ

NOW THE SERPENT WAS CLEVERER than all the animals the Lord God had made on the earth, and he said to the woman, So you think God said you mustn't eat the fruit of all the trees in the garden?

The woman said, We may eat the fruit of all the trees in the garden, except the tree in the middle of the garden. God said, You may not eat it, you may not touch it, or you will die.

The serpent said, You're not going to die! God only said that because He knows the day you eat that fruit, your eyes will be opened and you will be like God, and know everything, both good and evil.

The woman saw the fruit of the tree and it looked good to eat, and was beautiful, and would make her wise, and so she took the fruit and ate and gave some to her husband beside her, and he ate.

And the eyes of both were opened, and they understood that they were naked, so they braided fig leaves and covered themselves.

They heard the Lord God walking in the garden, in the cool of the day, and Adam and his wife hid from the Lord God among the trees in the garden.

And the Lord God called to Adam and said, Where are you?

Adam said, I heard You walking in the garden and was afraid, because I am naked, and so I hid myself.

The Lord said, Who told you that you were naked? Have you eaten the fruit of the tree I commanded you not to eat?

Adam said, The woman You gave me to be my companion—she gave me the fruit, and I ate.

The Lord God said to the woman, What have you done!

The woman said, The serpent tempted me, and I ate.

The Lord God said to the serpent, Because you have done this, you shall be most cursed among all the beasts upon the earth. Crawl on your stomach your life long! Eat dust! I shall make you enemies —you and the woman, and your children and her children. They will step on your head, and you will sting their heel.

To the woman He said, I shall multiply and increase the pain of your childbearing; in pain and sorrow shall you bear your children. You will yearn for your husband, and he will be your master.

To Adam He said, Because you obeyed the voice of your wife, and ate the fruit of the tree I commanded you not to eat, the earth will be cursed, because of you. In sorrow and in pain shall you get your nourishment out of the ground every day of your life. It will bear you thorns and thistles. You will eat the grain of the field; by the sweat of your brow shall you eat your bread till you return into the earth out of which you were taken, for dust is what you are and to dust you will return.

And the Lord God made tunics out of skins for Adam and his wife, and dressed them.

The Lord God said, This human has become like one of Us in the knowledge of all things, both good and evil. What if he reaches out his hand for the fruit of the tree of life as well, and becomes immortal!

And so the Lord God drove Adam out of the garden of Eden to plow the earth out of which he was taken, and banished

him from paradise. East of the garden He set angels with wheeling swords of fire to bar the way to the tree of life.

≈ ≈ ≈

AND ADAM AND HIS WIFE EVE lay together, and Eve conceived and bore Cain, and she conceived again and bore his brother Abel.

Abel became a shepherd, and Cain became a farmer and tilled the earth.

Time passed, and Cain brought the fruit of the earth as a burnt offering to the Lord, and Abel brought the fattest of the firstborn of his flock.

And the Lord accepted Abel and his offering, but He did not accept Cain, or his offering. And Cain was very angry and his face fell.

The Lord said to him, Why are you angry and why is your face fallen? If you walk with God you will be accepted, but if you go against God, evil lies in wait at the door, yearning for you. You will have to master it.

But Cain called his brother Abel, and when they were in the fields, Cain rose up and beat his brother to death.

And the Lord said to Cain, Where is your brother Abel?

Cain said, I don't know. Am I my brother's keeper?

The Lord said, What have you done! Listen! The voice of your brother's blood

And the time came when Cain built a city. Cain lay with his wife, and she conceived and bore a son, and Cain called him Enoch. And Cain called the city Enoch after his son. And the sons of Enoch lived in tents, kept sheep, and learned to play the zither and the lute, and to forge tools of copper and iron.

And Adam lay with his wife and she bore a son and called his name Seth, meaning God has given me another child instead of Abel, whom Cain slew.

≈ ≈ ≈

AND MEN BEGAN TO MULTIPLY on the earth, and the Lord saw that they were very wicked, and that everything they thought and imagined was always evil. Now the Lord was sorry He had made man on the earth and was grieved in His heart. He said, I shall destroy man, whom I have created, and every beast and every creeping thing and all the birds in the air. I wish that I had not made them.

Only Noah walked with God, in those days when God looked and saw nothing but corruption and violence wherever men moved on the earth.

And God said to Noah, I have determined to put an end to all living flesh. It fills the earth with violence. I shall destroy everything and the earth as well. Make yourself an ark out of gopher wood. Make rooms inside it and coat it with pitch inside and out. Make it four hundred and fifty feet long and seventy-five feet wide and forty-five feet high. Make a roof and put a window eighteen inches from the top. Make a door in the side and build a lower, a middle, and an upper deck.

cries to Me out of the ground. From this day on you are banished from the ground, which has opened its mouth to receive your brother's blood at your hands. It will grow you nothing. You shall wander without rest on the face of the earth.

And Cain said, My punishment is greater than I can bear. You have banished me from the ground and out of Your sight. I must wander without rest on the face of the earth, and whoever finds me will kill me.

But the Lord said, Whoever kills you shall be punished seven times over. And the Lord put a mark on Cain, so that those who met him would not kill him.

Cain went away from the Lord and lived in the land of Nod, east of Eden.

I shall send a flood that will destroy the earth and all living, breathing flesh. Everything that is on earth will go under. Only with you will I establish My covenant. You shall go into the ark—you and your sons and your wife and your sons' wives—and you shall take into the ark with you two of every living thing, one male and one female. Two of every kind of bird, and two of every kind of animal, and of every kind of thing that creeps on the earth, shall go into the ark with you to keep their kind alive.

Gather some of every kind of food and store it for nourishment for you and for them. In seven days from today I shall make it rain on the earth for forty days and forty nights and wipe every living thing that I have made off the face of the earth.

Noah did everything as the Lord commanded.

⁊ ⁊ ⁊

AND NOAH WAS SIX HUNDRED YEARS OLD when the flood came upon the earth, and the fountains of the great abyss burst open, the floodgates of heaven opened up, and Noah went into the ark with his sons, Shem, Ham, and Japheth, and his wife, and his sons' wives, and every kind of animal, and every kind of creeping thing, and every kind of chirping, flying bird. They went into the ark in twos, one male and one female, of every kind. Two of every kind of living thing that God had made came into the ark with Noah, and God closed the door behind him.

And the flood came, and it rained on the earth for forty days and forty nights.

The waters rose and lifted the ark. The waters swelled and rose and overran the earth, and the ark rode on the water. And still the waters rose and rose and covered the highest mountains under the heavens to a depth of twenty feet and more, until there was nothing to be seen on all the earth. All living flesh went under and everything that stirs on the earth, birds, cattle, wild animals, and everything that swarms upon the earth, and every man, and everything that breathes on the dry land died. Everything, every man and every beast and every creeping thing, and every bird under the heavens, was wiped off the earth.

Only Noah was left alive and what was with him in the ark, and the waters stood on the earth for one hundred and fifty days.

⁊ ⁊ ⁊

AND GOD REMEMBERED NOAH and all the living things that were in the ark with him and He sent a wind over the earth, and the waters fell. The fountains in the abyss were stopped up, the floodgates of the heavens closed, and the rains held back. The water began to run off the earth. It took one hundred and fifty days for the water to recede. On the seventeenth day of the seventh month the ark came to rest on Mount Ararat.

Noah waited forty days and then he opened the window and sent a raven out of the ark, and the raven flew to and fro over the earth until the water dried.

Then Noah sent out a dove to see if the water had receded, but the dove found no place to set the sole of her foot, because the water covered all the earth, and she came back to the ark, and Noah put out his hand and took the dove and brought her inside.

He waited seven more days and sent the dove out again, and she came, in the evening, and in her mouth she had the leaf of an olive! Then Noah knew the waters were receding. He waited seven more days and sent the dove out again, and she did not come back.

Still the waters fell, and the tops of the mountains appeared, and the water let go of the earth. Noah lifted the cover off the ark and, look! the earth was dry!

God said to Noah, Come out of the ark, you, your wife and your sons and their wives, and all the animals that are in the ark with you, and all the birds and everything that creeps; bring them out with you and let them swarm over the earth.

Noah came out with his sons and his wife and his sons' wives, and with all the animals and all the creeping things, all the birds and everything that moves on the earth, each of its own kind—they all came out of the ark.

Noah built an altar to the Lord and offered a burnt offering. The Lord smelled the sweet smell and in His heart He said, I will never again curse the earth on man's

account. The heart of man tends to evil from his childhood on, and will always be evil. As long as the earth remains, seedtime and harvest, frost and heat, summer and winter, day and night shall not cease on the earth.

And God blessed Noah and his sons, and said, Be fruitful, multiply and fill the earth. I give you everything that moves and lives to be food for you, just as I have given you the green plants. But you may not eat flesh with its lifeblood. You shall account to Me for every life—for your own life and for the life of your brother. If any man sheds another man's blood, his blood shall be shed in punishment, because God has made man in the likeness of God.

I shall establish My covenant with you and with your children after you, and with every living thing—with every bird and beast and all living things on the earth that came out of the ark with you. I shall set My rainbow into the clouds over the earth, and it shall be a sign of the covenant between Me and all the earth. Never again will the waters become a flood and destroy all flesh.

⚮ ⚮ ⚮

THE SONS OF NOAH, who came out of the ark with him, were Shem, Japheth, and Ham.

Noah was a farmer, the first to plant a vineyard, and Noah drank wine and became drunk and lay uncovered in his tent.

And Ham saw that his father was naked and told his brothers, but Shem and Japheth took a cloth, held it on their shoulders and, walking backward, they covered their father with their heads turned away, in order not to see their father's nakedness.

When Noah awoke from the wine, he cursed Ham and the sons of Ham, and blessed Shem and Japheth and their sons and said, May God bless Japheth and may He bless Shem, and may the sons of Ham be the slaves of the sons of Shem and Japheth.

And Noah lived three hundred and fifty years after the flood till he was nine hundred and fifty years old and then he died.

⚮ ⚮ ⚮

AND ALL THE PEOPLE spoke the same language and had the same words, and they came from the east and settled in the valley of Shinar.

They said to one another, Come, let us make bricks and bake them and use tar for mortar. We will build ourselves a city, and we will build a tower so high that it shall reach into the heavens. We will make a great name for ourselves so that we shall not be scattered over the face of the earth.

The Lord saw what they were doing and said, This is only the beginning. They are one people and speak one language. There is nothing they can think of that they will not be able to do. Come, let Us go down and confuse their language, so that they will not understand one another's words.

And the Lord came down and confused their language, and they did not finish the city. And the tower was called the Tower

of Babel, because the Lord confused the language of the world, and the people babbled, and did not understand one another's words and were scattered over the face of the earth.

≈ ≈ ≈

AND SHEM HAD A SON called Arpachshad who had a son Shelach who had a son Eber who had a son Peleg who had a son Reu who had a son Serug who had a son Nachor who had a son Terach. And Terach lived in the land of Ur and had three sons, Abraham, Nahor, and Haran. Haran had a son called Lot, and Haran died before his father's eyes. Abraham and Nahor took themselves wives. Abraham's wife was called Sarah and Nahor's wife was called Milcah. Sarah was barren and had no children.

And Terach took his son Abraham, and his grandson Lot, and Sarah, his daughter-in-law, the wife of his son Abraham, and set out from Ur for the land of Canaan, but when they came to Haran they settled there, and Terach lived two hundred and five years and died in Haran.

≈ ≈ ≈

NOW THE LORD SAID TO ABRAHAM, Leave your country, your family, and your father's house and go to a land that I will show you. I shall make you a great nation and bless you and bless those who bless you and curse those who curse you. You will become a blessing to the nations of the earth.

And Abraham did as the Lord said. Abraham was seventy-five years old when he left Haran. He took his wife Sarah, and his brother's son Lot went with him. They took their possessions and all their people and their herds and traveled west. And so they came to the land of Canaan and the Lord appeared to Abraham and said, This is the land that I will give to your children and your children's children.

And Abraham built an altar to the Lord in the place where the Lord appeared to him.

≈ ≈ ≈

AND THERE WAS A FAMINE in the land, and Abraham traveled down to stay in Egypt, because the famine in the land was very severe.

As he was about to enter Egypt, he said to his wife Sarah, Look, I know what a beautiful woman you are. When the Egyptians see you they will say, She is his wife, and they will kill me and will let you live. Say, I beg of you, that you are my sister, and then things will go well with me, for your sake, and I shall be let to live because of you.

And Abraham entered Egypt and the Egyptians saw the woman and how beautiful she was. The men of Pharaoh's court told Pharaoh about her, and she was brought to Pharaoh's palace. For her sake Abraham was treated well and got sheep and oxen and asses, menservants and maidservants, and she-asses and camels.

But the Lord afflicted Pharaoh and his household with great plagues, because of Abraham's wife Sarah. Pharaoh sent for Abraham and said, What have you done to me! Why didn't you tell me she was your wife? Why did you say, She is my sister, so that I took her to be my wife? Here! Here is your wife. Take her and go away. And Pharaoh gave his men charge over Abraham and sent him away with his wife and with all his possessions.

≈   ≈   ≈

AND ABRAHAM BECAME RICH in cattle, in silver, and in gold. Lot, too, had so many flocks and herds and tents that the land could not support the two living together in one place. There was quarreling among the herdsmen of Abraham's flocks and Lot's herdsmen. Abraham said, We cannot have this quarreling between you and me, and between your herdsmen and mine, for you and I are kinsmen. Look at the land that lies open before you. Let us part company. If you go left, I will go right, or if you want to go right, I will go left.

Lot looked up, and the plain of the river Jordan lay before him like a garden of the Lord, well watered, like the land of Egypt, so he chose the plain of the Jordan, and the two parted company. Abraham lived in Canaan and Lot went east to live among the cities of the plain and pitched his tents near Sodom. And the men of Sodom were wicked and great sinners in the eyes of the Lord.

After Lot had departed, the Lord said to Abraham, Look! Look around you! Look north and south and east and west. All the land that you can see I will give to you and your children and their children forever. I shall make your descendants as numerous as the grains of the dust on the earth. If a man could count the dust, he could count the number of your descendants.

But Abraham said, O Lord, my God, what good is anything that You give me? I have no children. My chief servant will inherit everything I own.

The Lord said, You shall have a son. And Abraham believed in the Lord.

≈   ≈   ≈

NOW ABRAHAM'S WIFE SARAH had an Egyptian slave girl and her name was Hagar. Sarah said to Abraham, The Lord has closed my womb; I cannot have children. Why don't you go in and lie with my slave Hagar. Maybe we can get a son by her.

And Sarah brought Hagar to her husband to get her husband a child. Abraham went in and lay with Hagar, and when Hagar saw that she was with child, she looked down on her mistress.

And Sarah said to Abraham, This is an injustice to me and it is your fault! I myself put my slave into your arms and now she sees she is with child and looks down on me!

Abraham said, She is your slave. Do what you think is right. But Sarah was so harsh with Hagar that Hagar ran away.

And the Lord sent His angel to find Hagar by a spring of water in the desert and said, Hagar, you are Sarah's slave. Where do you think you are going?

Hagar said, I am fleeing from my mistress Sarah.

The angel said, Go back. Put yourself in your mistress's hand. And the angel of the Lord said, Know that you will bear a son! Your son will be a wild sort of man.

He will be at war with everyone, and everyone will be at war with him. He and his brothers will be enemies. Know also that the Lord will so multiply your children and your children's children, they will be too many to count.

And Hagar went back to Sarah.

Abraham was eighty-six years old when Hagar, the Egyptian slave, bore him a son. She called the boy Ishmael, which means God saw my misery.

≈ ≈ ≈

ABRAHAM WAS NINETY-NINE YEARS OLD, and the Lord appeared to him and said, I am Almighty God. Walk in the way of the Lord. Be perfect. I shall make My covenant with you and make you very great.

And God said to Abraham, Let every male among you be circumcised. You shall cut your foreskin and it will be the sign of the covenant between Me and you.

God said, Know that you will be father of a multitude of nations! You will bring forth kings, and they will rule this land of Canaan into which you have come as a stranger. I shall give this land to your children and your children's children to be their everlasting possession, and I shall be their God.

Abraham fell to the ground before the Lord, but in his heart he laughed and said, I'm a hundred years old, and Sarah is ninety, and we're going to have a child?

And so Abraham said to the Lord, If you will only let my son Ishmael live in Your favor.

God said, I shall make him a great nation. But next year, when the time is ripe, Sarah too will bear you a son. Call him Isaac. It is with him I shall make My everlasting covenant, and with his children and his children's children after him.

And then He stopped talking and rose up, away from Abraham.

≈ ≈ ≈

AND THE LORD APPEARED TO ABRAHAM in Mamre as he sat at the door of his tent in the heat of the day. Abraham raised his eyes and there, in front of him, stood three men. He saw them and rose and ran toward them and bowed down to the ground and said, My Lord, show me that I have your favor and don't pass my tent without coming in! I'll have them bring a little water, and you can bathe your feet. Rest under my tree; I will bring you a little bread to eat. When you are refreshed you can go on your way. It is for this that your travels have brought you to your servant's tent.

They said, Well then, we will come in.

Abraham ran into the tent to Sarah and said, Quickly! Take three good measures of your finest flour and knead it and bake a cake. He ran out to the herd and chose a calf that was tender and good and gave it to a servant, who went quickly and cooked it. Abraham set butter and cream before his visitors and served them the good roast calf, but he himself remained standing under the tree.

They asked him, Where is your wife Sarah?

Abraham said, Inside, in the tent.

And the Lord said, I shall return when

the time is ripe, and your wife Sarah will have a son!

Sarah was listening at the door of the tent behind him and laughed in her heart and said, I am a worn-out old woman, and shall I have delight, now, when my husband too is an old man?

The Lord said, Why does Sarah laugh and say, How shall I, who am past childbearing, have a child? And then the Lord said, Is there anything so wonderful the Lord cannot make it happen? Sarah will bear a son.

Then Sarah denied it saying, I didn't laugh!—because she was afraid.

But the Lord said, Oh, yes, you did. You laughed.

≈ ≈ ≈

AND THE MEN ROSE and Abraham walked with them to see them on their way to Sodom.

And the Lord said to Himself, Shall I hide from Abraham what I am about to do? He will be father of a mighty nation, a blessing to the nations of the earth, because I have elected him to teach his children how to walk with the Lord, and practice mercy and justice. And the Lord said, A great outcry has come to Me against the wickedness of Sodom and Gomorrah. I will go down to see if their sins are as bad as the report says. If so, I shall destroy them; if not, I shall know it.

And the men left and went on their way to Sodom, but Abraham kept standing before the Lord and approached the Lord and said, Will You destroy the good together with the wicked? What if there are fifty good men in the city? Will You destroy it all the same? Will You not spare the city for the sake of fifty good men? Could You, the Judge of all the earth, judge so unjustly and kill the good with the wicked, as if there were no difference between goodness and wickedness?

The Lord said, If I find fifty good men in Sodom, I will forgive the whole city for their sake.

Abraham said, You see how I have taken it upon me to speak to my Lord—I, who am dust and ashes! What if there are five less than fifty good men? Will You destroy the whole city because of the five?

The Lord said, If I find forty-five good men I will not destroy the city.

But Abraham said, What if there are only forty?

The Lord said, Then I will not destroy it for the sake of the forty.

Abraham said, Lord, don't be angry because I'm still talking, but suppose there are only thirty?

The Lord said, I will spare them, if I find thirty.

Abraham said, Now I have dared to take it upon myself to speak, my Lord, what if You find only twenty?

The Lord said, I will not destroy the city if I find twenty.

And Abraham said, Please, don't be angry if I say one more thing! What if there are only ten?

The Lord said, I will not destroy the city for the sake of the ten.

And the Lord went away as soon as He had finished speaking with Abraham, and Abraham returned home.

≈ ≈ ≈

IN THE EVENING two angels arrived in Sodom. Now Lot lived near the city gates and looked up and rose and went toward them and bowed to the ground and said, O my good lords, come into your servant's house and rest for the night. Bathe your feet. Early tomorrow you can go on your way.

They answered, No, we can spend the night in the open.

But Lot pressed them, and they came into his house. He gave them food and drink, and they were about to go to bed when the men of the city of Sodom, the young men as well as the old, every last one of them, came and surrounded the house, and they called to Lot and said, Where are these men who came into your house tonight? Bring them out to us so we can have our fun with them.

Lot went out to them and closed the door behind him and said, You must not do these wicked things, my brothers! Look, I have two daughters, who have never lain with any man. I shall bring them out to you; do with them what you want, but you must not touch these men, for they are guests under my roof.

But the men of Sodom said, Out of our way! Here's a fellow, and a stranger in our town, laying down the law to us! We're going to do worse things to you than anything we do to them!

And they crowded in on Lot and would have broken down the door, but the men inside reached their hand out and drew Lot into the house and locked the door. Those outside were blinded with confusion, the young and the old, and

tired themselves out trying to find the door.

And now the men said, If you have kinfolk in the city, a son-in-law or sons or daughters, get them out of town. The Lord has heard the outcry against the great wickedness of the people of Sodom and Gomorrah and has sent us to destroy them.

Lot went out and said to his sons-in-law, Quick! Leave the city! The Lord is going to destroy it. Lot's sons-in-law thought he was joking.

When morning came, the angels of the Lord tried to hurry Lot and said, Quick! Take your wife and the two daughters who live with you, or you will be destroyed in the destruction of this wicked city.

Still Lot hung back, so the men took him by the hand, and took the hands of his wife and his two daughters, because God wanted to save them, and they led them away and did not let go of them until they were outside the gates. They said, Flee for your life. Do not look back. Get out of the plain. Go up into the mountains and save yourself.

But Lot said, Oh, my Lord, no! Your great goodness has spared Your servant's life, but I wouldn't be safe in the mountains! Something terrible will happen to me, and I shall die! There is a little town quite near. It is called Zoar. I could flee there. It's quite a little town, and I could be safe there. You see how tiny it is!

The Lord said, This, too, I will do for you. I will spare that little town, only hurry! I can't do anything till you are safe.

The sun rose on the earth as Lot entered the little town of Zoar. Now the Lord rained fire and brimstone from the heavens down upon Sodom and Gomorrah and destroyed the cities and all the plain, and all who lived in the cities and everything that grew in the land.

And Lot's wife, who came behind him, looked back and was turned into a pillar of salt.

And Abraham rose early in the morning and went to the place where he had stood before the Lord. He looked across the land of Sodom and Gomorrah and saw smoke rise from the plain like the smoke that rises from an oven.

And so it was that God destroyed the cities of the plain, but remembered Abraham and saved Lot from calamity when He destroyed the city in which Lot lived.

꼭 꼭 꼭

AND LOT LEFT ZOAR and lived in the mountains, together with his two daughters, because he was afraid to stay in Zoar. He lived in a cave, he and his two daughters.

And the older daughter said to the younger, Our father is old, and there is no other man in the world to come in and lie with us, as it is done all over the world. Come, let us make our father drink wine and let's lie with him and continue life through our father's seed.

On that same night they made their father drink wine and the older went in and lay with her father and he was not aware when she lay down or when she got up.

In the morning the older daughter said to the younger, Look, last night I lay with my father. Let's make him drink wine again, tonight, and you go in and lie with him, so that life will continue through our father's seed. And they made their father drink wine again and that night the younger daughter went in and lay down with her father. And he was not aware when she lay down or when she got up.

And so Lot's two daughters were with child by their father. The older had a son, and called him Moab, meaning fatherseed, who is father of the Moabites of today. The younger daughter had a son, and called him Ben-Ammi, meaning my kin's son, who became the father of the Ammonites of today.

℞ ℞ ℞

AND GOD REMEMBERED SARAH and the promise He had made her and did what He had said. Sarah conceived and when the time was ripe she bore Abraham a son. Abraham called him Isaac, and circumcised him when he was eight days old.

Abraham was a hundred years old when his son Isaac was born.

Sarah said, God has brought me laughter in my old age, and everyone who hears about this will laugh because of me! Who could have thought Sarah would nurse a child! Here have I borne Abraham a son in his old age!

The child grew and was weaned, and on the day of Isaac's weaning Abraham made a great feast.

But Sarah looked at Ishmael, the son whom Hagar, her Egyptian slave, had borne Abraham, and the boy was laughing and playing, and Sarah said to Abraham, Get rid of the woman and her son. A slave's son shall never share my son's inheritance.

Her words grieved Abraham, because of the boy, but God said, Do not grieve for the boy or for the woman. Do what Sarah says.

Abraham rose early in the morning and took bread and a flask of water, and he put it and the child on Hagar's shoulders and sent them away.

Hagar wandered about the desert of Beersheba and when the water in the flask was gone, she laid the child under the shade of a bush and sat down as far away as a bow will shoot an arrow, because she could not bear to watch him die. And Hagar lifted up her voice and wept.

But God heard the voice of the child crying, and God's angel called to Hagar out of heaven, and said, What is it, Hagar? Don't be afraid. God has heard the boy where he lies. Come, get up, take the child by the hand. I will make him into a great nation. And Hagar looked up and God opened her eyes and she saw a well of water and she filled the flask and gave it to the boy to drink.

Ishmael grew up in the desert and became a great archer, and his mother found him a wife from among her people in Egypt.

≈ ≈ ≈

AND THERE CAME A TIME after Abraham sent Hagar away, when God tested Abraham and said, Abraham!

Abraham said, Here I am.

God said, Take your son, your only son, the one you love, Isaac, and go into the land of Moriah and offer him to Me as a burnt offering on the mountain which I will show you.

Abraham rose early in the morning and saddled his ass, and took two of his servants and his son Isaac. He chopped the wood for the burnt offering and set out for the place of which God had told him.

On the third day Abraham looked up and saw the place from afar. He said to his servants, Stay here with the ass. I and the boy will go and worship and come back to you.

Abraham took the wood for the burnt offering and put it on Isaac's shoulders. The fire and the knife he carried in his own hand, and the two walked together.

Isaac said, my father!

Abraham said, Here I am, my son.

Isaac said, We have the fire and the wood, but where is the lamb for the burnt offering?

Abraham said, God will provide Himself a lamb for the burnt offering, my son.

And the two walked together. They came to the place of which God had told him, and Abraham built an altar and arranged the wood, and bound Isaac his son and laid him on the altar, on top of the wood. And Abraham stretched out his hand and took the knife to slaughter his son, and the Lord's angel called to him out of heaven, and said, Abraham! Abraham!

Abraham said, Here I am.

And He said, Don't lay a hand on the boy and do him no hurt. Now I know that you fear God, because you did not deny Me your son, your only son.

Abraham looked up and saw a ram with its horns caught in the thicket behind him, and Abraham took the ram and offered it upon the altar in his son's stead.

And God's angel called down to Abraham a second time out of heaven and said, This I swear to you by My Self—because you have not denied Me your son, your only son, I shall bless you and make you numerous as the stars in the sky and as the sand on the seashore. Your children shall inherit the cities of their enemies and in your posterity shall the nations of the earth be blessed, for you heard My voice and obeyed it.

Then Abraham returned to his servants, and they set off together and returned to Beersheba.

℀ ℀ ℀

AND SARAH WAS one hundred and twenty-seven years old and died in Hebron, in the land of Canaan, and Abraham came to mourn for Sarah and to weep for her.

And he rose from beside his dead wife and spoke to the Hittites and said, I am a stranger living among you. Give me a burial place here so that I can bury my dead.

The Hittites said, If you please, my lord, you are a prince of God among us. Choose yourself the best of our burial places. There's not a man among us who will deny you his own place for you to bury your dead.

Abraham bowed down to these Hittites and said to them, Since you are willing to let me bury my dead among you, speak for me, I beg you, to Ephron, the son of Zohar, to sell me the cave of Machpelah which he owns. It's at the far end of his field. Ask him to sell it to me at the full price so that I shall have a burial place among you.

Ephron was there among the Hittites, and Ephron began to bargain with Abraham in the hearing of all the townspeople within the town gate, and said, Not at all, my lord, I will give you the field, and the cave in it. In the presence of all the people I give it into your possession. Go and bury your dead.

Abraham bowed down before the people and spoke to Ephron so that all could hear him, and said, Not at all, my lord! But since you say that you are willing to give it to me, I beg of you, let me give you the money to pay for the field.

Accept the money from me so that I may bury my dead in it.

And Ephron answered Abraham and said, Oh, but my lord, if you please, the land is worth a mere four hundred shekels of silver. What is that between you and me? Go and bury your dead.

And Abraham accepted Ephron's offer and weighed out to him, in the presence of all the Hittites within the city gates, four hundred pieces of silver, according to the weight current among merchants.

And so Ephron's land in Machpelah, near Mamre, the field with its cave and all the trees that grew within the borders of that field, passed that day, and in the hearing of all the Hittites within the city gate, once and for all, into the possession of Abraham, a stranger in the land.

And Abraham buried his wife Sarah in the cave in the field of Machpelah, near Mamre, which we now call Hebron. And that is how the field and the cave in it were deeded to be Abraham's possession as a burial place in the land of Canaan.

℀ ℀ ℀

NOW ABRAHAM WAS AN OLD MAN, well on in years, and the Lord had blessed him and everything that was his.

And Abraham said to the eldest of his servants, who had charge of his household: Put your hand under my thigh, I beg you, and I will make you swear by the Lord, the God of heaven and earth, that you will not choose my son a wife from the daughters of the Canaanites, among whom we live. Go into my own country, to my own people, and bring back a wife for Isaac.

The servant said, What if the woman will not come with me? Shall I take Isaac back to the land from which you came?

Abraham said, Never take my son back! The Lord, who brought me out of my father's house and out of my native land and swore to give the land of Canaan to my children, will send His angel before you. You will find my son a wife. If the woman will not come back with you, you are released from this oath. Only swear never to take my son back there.

And so the servant put his hand under his master Abraham's thigh and swore and he took ten of his master's camels and some of his master's treasure and set out for Mesopotamia, and came to Haran.

He made the camels kneel down by the well outside the town. It was evening, the time when the women of the town came out to draw water. He said, O Lord, God of my master Abraham, I stand here, by this well, and the daughters of the town are coming to draw water. Now if a girl comes, and I say to her, Tilt your jug and let me drink!—and she says, Drink, and I will draw water so your camels can drink too!—let her be the wife whom You have chosen for my master's son Isaac.

Before he had finished speaking there came Rebekah, the daughter of Bethuel, the son of Milcah and Nahor, Abraham's brother. She carried a jug on her shoulder. She was a beautiful girl, and a virgin. She went down to the well and filled her jug, and the servant ran toward her and said, Give me a drink of water from your jug.

She said, Drink, my lord!—and quickly took the jug from her shoulder, and when he had drunk his fill, she said, I will draw water for your camels too, so they can drink their fill.

She emptied her jug into the trough, and ran back to the well and drew more water, and watered all his camels.

The man watched in silence and marveled, waiting to know if the Lord had given his journey a good outcome or not. When the camels had drunk their fill, he took out a golden nose ring and gave it to the girl and gave her two gold bracelets and said, Tell me, who is your father? Is there room in your father's house, so that we might stay the night?

She said, I am the daughter of Bethuel, the son of Milcah and Nahor. We have a lot of straw and fodder, and room for you to stay the night.

Now the man bowed down and worshipped the Lord and said, Praise to the Lord, God of my master Abraham, who has guided my path to the house of my master's brother!

The girl ran home to her mother's house and told them everything that had happened.

Rebekah had a brother, and his name was Laban. When he saw the nose ring, and the bracelets on his sister's arms, he ran out to find the man, who stood by the well with his camels. And Laban said, Why are you standing out here? I have made the house ready for you and there's room for your camels too.

The man came into the house and unloaded the camels, and they brought straw and feed and water for the man and for all the men who had come with him, to bathe their feet.

And they set food before him, but the servant said, I will not eat until I have told my errand.

They said, Then tell it.

The man said, I am Abraham's servant. The Lord has blessed my master, and he has grown great and rich in sheep and cattle and silver and gold, menservants and maidservants, and camels and asses. My master's wife Sarah bore him a son in her old age, and he will inherit everything. My master has made me swear to bring back a wife for his son Isaac from his own people. Today, when I came to the well, I said, God of my master Abraham, give my journey a good outcome! Here I stand, by the well. Let it happen that the girl who comes to draw water, to whom I shall say, Give me a sip of water from your jug!—and who says, Drink your fill, and I will draw water for your camels too!—let her be the wife whom You have chosen for my master's son Isaac! And before I had finished speaking there came Rebekah with her jug on her shoulder, and I said, Give me a drink of water! And she quickly took the jug from her shoulder and said, Drink, and I will draw water for your camels too! And I bowed down and worshipped the Lord, who had guided my path to the daughter of my master's brother, to be his son's wife. Now, if you mean to act kindly and fairly by my master, tell me. If not, I must see what to do next.

They said, This is the work of the Lord. It's not for us to say that it is good or bad. Here stands Rebekah before you. Take her and go. Let her be the wife of your master's son. It is the Lord's will.

When Abraham's servant heard this, he bowed down to the ground and worshipped the Lord. He took out treasures of gold and of silver, and clothing, and gave them to Rebekah, and to her brother and to her mother, a bride price of costly presents. And they ate and drank, and he and the men who had come with him stayed overnight. In the morning they rose, and he said, Let me be on my way home to my master.

Rebekah's brother and her mother said, Let her stay a little while longer, and then you can go.

The servant said, Don't hold me here. Let me start the journey back to my master.

They said, Let us call the girl and ask her.

They called Rebekah and asked her, Will you go with this man?

Rebekah said, I will go.

And they blessed Rebekah and said, Dear sister! May you be the mother of thousands of millions, and may your children's children inherit the cities of their enemies!

And Rebekah and her nurse and her maids got ready and mounted the camels and went with the man and the men who had come with him.

Now Isaac had come out, at evening time, to walk in the field and to think, and he looked up and saw camels coming toward him.

Rebekah, too, looked up and saw Isaac and she got off her camel. She asked the servant, Who is that man in the field, walking toward us?

The servant said, That is my master.

Rebekah took her veil and covered herself.

And the servant told Isaac all he had accomplished. Isaac brought Rebekah into his mother's tent and she became his wife, and he loved her and found comfort after his mother's death.

And Abraham lived to be a hundred and seventy-five years and died contented and full of years, and his sons Isaac and Ishmael buried him in the cave in the field with his wife Sarah.

≈ ≈ ≈

ISAAC WAS FORTY YEARS when he took Rebekah to be his wife, and Isaac prayed to the Lord because Rebekah was barren. And the Lord heard Isaac's prayer, and Rebekah conceived, but the children struggled with one another in her womb. Rebekah went to consult with the Lord and said, What is happening, and what does it mean?

The Lord said, There are two nations in your womb. Two peoples will be born out of your body. One will be mightier than the other, and the older shall serve the younger.

When her time came Rebekah gave birth to twins. The first came out covered with red as with a coat of fur. They called him Esau, meaning hairy. After him came his brother with his hand holding Esau's heel, and they called him Jacob, which means heel holder.

Isaac was sixty years old when they were born.

༂ ༂ ༂

THE BOYS GREW, and Esau became a skillful hunter, a man who lived out in the open, but Jacob was quiet and stayed at home among the tents.

Isaac loved Esau because he took pleasure in the taste of the wild game that his son brought home from the hunt, but Rebekah loved Jacob best.

One day, Jacob was cooking stew and Esau came in from the field weak with hunger and said, Quick! Feed me some of that red stuff to swallow down. I'm dying of hunger.

Jacob said, First sell me your birthright as the eldest son.

Esau said, What good is my birthright if I'm dead with hunger?

Jacob said, Swear to sell it to me.

And so Esau swore to sell his birthright to his brother Jacob, and Jacob gave Esau bread and lentil stew, and Esau ate and drank and went on his way. That is how little Esau thought of his birthright.

༂ ༂ ༂

AND THE TIME CAME when Isaac grew old; his eyes were weak and he could not see. He called his older son Esau.

Esau said, Here I am.

Isaac said, You see, I'm an old man. The day will come when I must die. Go, get your bow and quiver. Hunt me some wild game and cook it the way I like and bring it to me. I shall eat it and give you my heart's blessing before I die.

Rebekah heard Isaac speaking with Esau. When Esau was gone hunting, she said to Jacob, I heard your father speaking with your brother Esau. He said, Bring me some game, cook it the way I like, and I will eat it and give you my heart's blessing before I die. Now listen to me, my son, and do what I tell you. Go out to the herd. Bring me two fine young goats. I will cook the meal your father likes, and you will take it to your father. He will eat it and give you his blessing before he dies.

Jacob said, My brother Esau is a hairy man, and my skin is smooth. If my father touches me, I shall stand there like a trickster and bring down his curse upon me, not his blessing.

His mother said, Let the curse fall on me, my son. Do as I tell you. Go and get the goats.

Jacob went and got the goats and brought them to his mother, who cooked them the way his father liked. Then she took her older son's favorite clothes, which she kept in the house, and put them on Jacob, and covered his hands and his hairless neck with the skins of the goats,

and gave him the good food that she had cooked to carry to his father.

Jacob went in to his father and said, Father!

Isaac said, I am here, and who are you, my son?

Jacob said, I am Esau, your firstborn. I have done what you said. Will you sit up and eat my venison and give me your heart's blessing?

Isaac said, How quickly you found it, my son!

Jacob said, The Lord your God saw to it.

Isaac said, Come closer. If I touch you I shall know if you really are my son Esau or not.

Jacob came to his father and Isaac touched him and said, The voice is the voice of Jacob but the hands are Esau's hands. And he did not know that it was Jacob, because of his hairy hands, which were like his brother Esau's hands, and he said, Are you really my son Esau?

Jacob said, I am.

Isaac said, Come, give me the meat from the hunt so that I may eat it and give you my heart's blessing.

Jacob gave his father the food, and Isaac ate, and he brought him wine, and he drank.

Then Isaac said, Come here, my son, and kiss me. And Jacob kissed him. Isaac smelled his clothes and blessed him and said, Ah, the smell of my son is the smell of a field which the Lord has blessed. May God give you of the fat of the land and the dew of heaven, and plenty of corn and wine. Nations shall serve you and bow down before you. I make you lord over your brothers. Your mother's sons shall bow themselves down. A curse on those who curse you and a blessing on those who bless you.

When Isaac finished the blessing, Jacob left his father's presence, and now Esau came in from the hunt. He, too, cooked his father's favorite meal and brought it to him and said, Will you sit up, Father, and eat the meat I have brought home from the hunt, and give me your heart's blessing?

His father said, Who are you?

He said, I am your son, your firstborn, Esau!

And Isaac shook with a terrible trembling and said, Who was it, then, who brought me meat from the hunt that I ate before you came! It is him that I blessed, and blessed he will remain!

Esau heard what his father said and shouted aloud and cried bitterly and said, Father, bless me too!

But Isaac said, Your brother has cheated you out of your blessing.

Esau said, It's not for nothing he is called Jacob, the Heel Holder! Doubly underhanded, he took hold of my birthright, and now he has hold of my blessing too! Is there no blessing left, Father, for me?

Isaac said, I have made him lord over you and have given him his brothers to be his servants, and corn and wine to be his sustenance. What is there left to give to you?

Esau cried, Do you have only one blessing! Me, too, Father! Bless me, too! And Esau wept aloud.

Isaac said, By the sword shall you live and serve your brother, but a time will come when you will bestir yourself and shake off his yoke.

From that day forward Esau hated Jacob. In his heart he said, The day is near when we will mourn my father. Afterward I will kill my brother Jacob.

They told Rebekah what her older son had said, and she sent word to Jacob, Your brother Esau is full of thoughts of vengeance. He wants to kill you. Do what I tell you. Flee to my brother Laban. Stay with him until your brother's fury has had time to cool. When he forgets what you have done to him, I'll send you word and you can return. Why should I lose both my sons on the same day?

To Isaac, Rebekah said, These Hittite women sicken me. If Jacob takes a wife from among the women of this land, my life is not worth living.

Isaac called for Jacob and said, Don't take a local woman to be your wife.

Get yourself ready, go east, and find yourself a wife from among the daughters of Laban, your mother's brother. So Isaac sent Jacob away.

≈ ≈ ≈

JACOB SET OUT FROM BEERSHEBA and traveled east toward Haran, and came to a certain place, and stayed the night because the sun had already set. And Jacob took a stone that lay there and put it under his head for a pillow and he lay down and slept and dreamed he saw a ladder set upon the earth, and its top reached into heaven. He saw the angels of God ascending and descending, and at the top stood the Lord and said, I am the God of Abraham and the God of Isaac. To you and to your children shall I give the land on which you lie asleep. Your children will be like the dust of the earth. They will spread west and east and north and south. The nations of the earth will be blessed because of you, for I am with you. I shall watch over you wherever you go. I shall bring you home to this land and not leave you until I have accomplished the promise that I give to you.

Jacob awoke out of his sleep and said, Surely the Lord is in this place, and I did not know it! And he was filled with dread and said, How full of dread is this place! What can it be except the house of God, and here is the gate to heaven.

And Jacob rose early in the morning and took the stone that he had put under his head and set it up as a pillar and anointed it with oil and called the place Bethel, which means the House of God.

And Jacob made a vow and said, If

God is with me on this journey, and gives me bread to eat and a coat to wear and I return safely to my father's house, then He shall be my God. This pillar shall be the temple of the Lord. Of everything You give me I shall set aside a tenth part for You!

≈ ≈ ≈

AND JACOB PICKED HIMSELF up and continued his journey to Haran. And Jacob came to a field and looked about him and there was a well, and a big stone covered the mouth of the well. Three flocks of sheep lay nearby, waiting to be watered.

Jacob asked the shepherds, Where do you come from, my brothers?

They said, We're from Haran.

He said, Do you know Laban, the son of Nahor?

They said, Yes, we know him.

Jacob asked, Is he well?

They said, He is well, and here comes his daughter Rachel with her father's sheep.

Jacob said to them, The sun is still high, and it's too early to take in the flocks. Why don't you water them and take them back into the pasture?

They said, We cannot water them until all the shepherds have come. Then we can roll away the stone, water the sheep, and set the stone back in its place.

While Jacob was talking with the shepherds, Rachel came up with her father's sheep, for she was a shepherdess. And Jacob saw her and Jacob went to the well and rolled away the stone, and watered his uncle's sheep. And Jacob kissed Rachel and wept aloud. Jacob told

her he was her father's kin, Rebekah's son. And Rachel ran and told her father.

Laban came out to meet Jacob. He embraced him and kissed him and brought him into the house, and Jacob told Laban all that had happened.

And Laban said, You are my flesh and blood indeed!

Jacob stayed a month with Laban, and Laban said, Why should you work for nothing though you are my sister's son? Tell me what I should pay you.

Now Laban had two daughters. The older was called Leah, and Rachel was the younger. Leah had pale eyes, but Rachel was lovely in figure and face, and Jacob loved her. He said, I will serve you seven years for your younger daughter Rachel.

Laban said, I'd rather give her to you than to a stranger. Stay with me.

Jacob served seven years for Rachel, and they seemed to him like a few days because he loved her. Then Jacob said, I have served out my seven years. Give me my wife and I will go in and lie with her.

Laban invited all the people in the place and made a feast. He gave his maidservant Zilpah to his older daughter Leah to be her maid and he took Leah, veiled her like a bride, and brought her in to Jacob, and Jacob lay with her.

Morning came, and there was Leah!

Jacob went to Laban and said, You've tricked me! It was Rachel for whom I worked for seven years. Why have you cheated me?

Laban said, We don't do that here— give the younger in marriage before the firstborn. Fulfill your bridal week with your wife, then we will give you the

younger, too, if you agree to serve me another seven years for her.

Jacob fulfilled his week with Leah, and Laban gave him his younger daughter Rachel to be his wife, and he gave Rachel his maidservant Bilhah to be her maid. Jacob went in and lay with Rachel, too, and he loved Rachel better than he loved Leah. And Jacob continued in Laban's service.

≍   ≍   ≍

THE LORD SAW that Leah was not beloved and He opened her womb, but Rachel, who was beloved, was barren and did not bear Jacob children.

Leah conceived and bore a son and called him Reuben, and said, The name means the Lord sees my unhappiness. Now my husband will love me!

And she conceived again and bore a son and called him Simeon and said, It means the Lord hears that I am still unloved, therefore He has given me another son.

She conceived again and bore a son and said, This time my husband will become attached to me, for I have borne him three sons! And she called the child Levi, which means attached.

She conceived again and bore a fourth son and said, I shall praise the Lord and keep hoping! And she named the boy Judah, meaning praise, and after that she bore no more children.

Rachel saw that she did not bear Jacob any children and envied her sister Leah and said to Jacob, Give me children or I shall die!

Jacob became angry too and said, Do I stand in the place of God? Is it I who deny you children?

Rachel said, Take my maid Bilhah. Go in and lie with her and she shall bear you a son on my lap and I shall rear him as my own. And Rachel gave her husband Jacob her servant Bilhah to be his wife and Jacob went in and lay with her, and she conceived and bore him a son.

Rachel said, God has given me His judgment! He has given me a son! She called the child Dan, meaning judge.

And Rachel's servant Bilhah conceived again and bore Jacob a second son. Rachel said, I have wrestled with my sister and have won! She named the child Naphtali, meaning wrestler.

When Leah saw that she had stopped bearing, she gave Jacob her maidservant Zilpah to be his wife, and Zilpah bore Jacob a son. Leah called him Gad, meaning good fortune.

And Leah's servant Zilpah bore Jacob a second son, and Leah called him Asher, meaning happiness.

And it was in the days of harvest that Reuben went out into the fields and found a mandrake and brought it to his mother Leah.

Rachel said, Please, give me your son's mandrake!

Leah said, It isn't enough that you have taken my husband, now you want my son's mandrake too?

Rachel said, If you give me your son's mandrake, my husband shall lie with you tonight.

In the evening, when Jacob came in from the fields, Leah went out to meet him and said, You must lie with me tonight. I have paid for you with my son's mandrake.

And Jacob lay with her that night. Leah conceived and bore Jacob a fifth son and called the child Issachar, which means repayment.

And Leah conceived again and bore Jacob a sixth son and said, He is a precious gift and now, at last, my husband will honor me. I have borne him six sons! And she called the child Zebulun, meaning precious gift.

And she bore Jacob a daughter and called her Dinah.

And God remembered Rachel, and God heard her prayer and opened her womb. Rachel conceived and bore Jacob a son and said, God has taken away my shame! She called the child Joseph, and said, May the Lord give me another son!

≈   ≈   ≈

AFTER RACHEL BORE JOSEPH, Jacob went to Laban and said, Release me from my service. Let me go home to my own country and take my wives and children for whom I have served you twenty years.

Laban said, Show me your good favor and stay with me. I know it's for your sake that the Lord has blessed me. Name your wages. I will pay you.

Jacob said, You know the service I have done you—how small your herd was before I came and how it has increased and grown under my care. The Lord has blessed your household because of me.

Isn't it time that I provide for my own household?

Laban said, Only tell me what I shall give you.

Jacob said, Give me nothing. I will go back and I will tend your flocks, if you agree to let me set aside the few speckled sheep and goats and they shall be my only wages. My honesty shall speak for me: If there's a sheep or goat found in my possession that is not speckled or mottled, you shall consider it stolen.

Laban said, Very well. We'll do as you say.

Jacob went that very day and separated out the striped and speckled males, and the speckled and the mottled females, every animal with any white on it, and Jacob tended Laban's herd. Now Jacob cut green poplar branches. He peeled off the bark to show the white inside and put these striped, speckled, and mottled branches in the troughs, where Laban's flocks came to drink. The animals that faced the branches while they mated bore him striped, speckled, and mottled young, and Jacob took them for his own. From that day on Jacob took the strong, healthy animals, made them face the speckled branches, and they bore speckled young, which he took for his own, and the weak and old animals he did not face toward the branches and they bore young that were not speckled, and belonged to Laban's herd. And Jacob's herd increased and he grew very rich in animals and maidservants and menservants, and camels and asses.

And Jacob heard Laban's sons saying, Jacob takes everything our father owns and makes himself rich. And Jacob looked at Laban and Laban did not look at him as kindly as before.

The Lord said to Jacob, Go home to your own people. I shall be with you.

Jacob sent for Rachel and Leah to come to him in the fields and said, Your father does not look at me as kindly as before, but the Lord is with me. You know I have served your father with all my strength, and he has tricked me and cheated me out of my wages ten times over. God has kept him from doing me harm. If your father says, The speckled animals shall be your wages!—then the herds have speckled young. If he says, The striped shall be your wages!—then the flocks bear me striped young. God takes the animals from your father and gives them to me. The angel of God has called to me in a dream. I said, Here I am! And He said, Look how all the males that mate are striped, speckled, and mottled! I have seen how Laban cheats you. I am the God of Bethel. Leave this land and go back to your people!

Rachel and Leah said, We have no share in our father's wealth. He treats us like foreigners. He sold us and used up our purchase price and more. What God has taken from our father belongs to us and to our children. Do as God says.

Now Jacob put his children and his wives on the camels, said nothing to Laban, and drove his herds ahead of him, and all his possessions that he had gained in Haran, and set out for the land of Canaan, crossed the Euphrates, and pitched his tents in the hills of Gilead.

Now Rachel had stolen the household

gods out of her father's house and brought them with her, and Jacob did not know.

On the third day Laban saw Jacob had fled and took his kinfolk and pursued Jacob into the hills of Gilead and pitched his tents. And God came to Laban in a dream and said, Let Jacob alone. Say nothing to him, neither good nor bad.

Laban caught up with Jacob and said, How could you do such a thing? You steal away my heart when you carry off my daughters like captives of war! Why did you flee in the dark? I would have seen you off with singing and the sound of tambourines and harps! You did not let me kiss the children and my daughters good-bye. And it was foolish of you. I have it in my power to hurt you. But last night the God of your father spoke to me in a dream and said, Let Jacob alone. Say nothing to him, neither good nor bad. And Laban said, If you want to leave, go! You want to return to your father's house, very well, but why do you steal my household gods?

Jacob said, I left because I was afraid you would take your daughters back by force, but if there is anybody here who has stolen your household gods, that person shall die! Search us in the presence of all your kinfolk; if you find anything of yours, take it.

Laban went into Jacob's tent and into Leah's tent and the tent of the two maid-servants, and found nothing. He went into Rachel's tent, but Rachel took the household gods and put them in the saddle on her camel and sat on them. To her father she said, My lord must excuse me that I do not rise in your presence, but it is my time and I am unwell today.

Laban searched and did not find his household gods.

Now Jacob was angry and quarreled with Laban and said, What was my crime? What wrong did I ever do you that you should hunt me down? You have rummaged through my things and have you found any of your household stuff? If so, tell me here, before your kinfolk and mine, and let them judge between us! I have served you these twenty years, and you and all your sheep and goats have not miscarried. I never ate one ram belonging to your flocks nor brought you what the wild beasts tore, but have made good the loss myself, though you demanded pay-ment from me for what was stolen, day or night. How have I lived the while? The day's heat and the night's frost con-sumed me. Sleep fled my eyes. Twenty years I worked in your household. I served you fourteen years for your two daughters, six years for your sheep, and you have changed my wages ten times over. If it were not for my fathers' God you never would have let me go. He has seen my hardship and my labor, and last night He rebuked you in your dream!

Laban said, These daughters are my daughters, these children are my children, the sheep are my sheep. Everything you see here, it's all mine! As for my daughters —there's nothing I can do about them now, or about these children they have borne! Come now! Let us make a cove-nant, you and I. These stones shall be our witnesses. Let the Lord witness between you and me when we can no longer watch each other: If you mistreat my daughters or take yourself other wives, remember, God is our witness!

And Jacob took an oath and offered a burnt offering. They invited their kinfolk to the feast and slept the night on the hills. Early in the morning Laban kissed his grandchildren and his daughters and blessed them and returned home.

≈ ≈ ≈

AND JACOB TRAVELED ON toward Canaan and sent his messengers ahead to his brother Esau to say, Your lordship's servant, your brother Jacob, has sent us to your lordship. Your brother says, I have been Laban's guest all this while and have grown rich in cattle and asses, sheep and goats, menservants and maidservants. I send this message to your lordship in the hope of your lordship's favor!

The messengers returned and said, We saw your brother Esau. He is coming toward you with four hundred men.

And now Jacob was afraid and divided his people and his herds and camels in two camps and said, if Esau attacks one camp, the other may be saved! And he said, God of my father Abraham, and of my father Isaac! You said to me, Go back to your own land and your own people! Lord, I am not worthy of the faithful kindness You have shown Your servant, but I am afraid my brother will attack me and the mothers with their children. You said to me, I will deal kindly with you and make you great. Your children and their children shall be numerous as the sand on the seashore, which no man can count! Save me now from my brother Esau!

And Jacob stayed the night, and he chose two hundred she-goats and twenty he-goats, two hundred ewes and twenty rams, thirty milk camels with their young, forty cows and ten bulls, twenty female asses and ten males, and sent them ahead as presents to his brother Esau. He put them in the charge of his servants, one herd to each servant, and said, Walk ahead of me and keep a distance between one herd and the next.

To the one who went first he said, When you meet my brother Esau and he asks, Whose men are you? Where are you going? Whose are these herds?—you must say, The herd belongs to your servant Jacob, who has sent it as a present to your lordship, and he himself is not far behind us.

He said the same thing to the second, and to the third and to the other servants who followed with the other herds, saying, You must all say the same thing when you meet Esau, and each of you must say, Your servant Jacob is coming right behind us.

For Jacob said to himself, If he is pleased with my presents he might be pleased to see me! And so Jacob sent his presents ahead of him.

That night Jacob sent his two wives, his two maidservants, and eleven sons across the river Jabbok and sent across

everything he owned. And Jacob was left alone, and a man wrestled with him until the break of day. When the man saw that he did not overcome Jacob, he touched the socket of his thigh, and Jacob's thigh was put out of joint, wrestling with the man.

The man said, Let me go, for the day breaks.

Jacob said, I will not let you go until you bless me.

The man said, What is your name?

He said, Jacob.

Then the man said, Your name is no longer Jacob; your name shall be Israel, who wrestles with God, because you wrestle with God and with men and you conquer.

Jacob said, Tell me your name!

But He said, Why do you ask me my name? And He blessed him.

And Jacob called the place Peniel, meaning I have seen God face to face, and yet my life was saved!

And the sun rose above Jacob as he passed Peniel, limping because of his hip.

ᴁ ᴁ ᴁ

AND JACOB RAISED HIS EYES, and look! There came Esau with his four hundred men! Jacob approached his brother and bowed to the ground seven times, but Esau came running and threw his arms around his brother's neck, embraced and kissed him, and they wept together. Esau looked and saw the women and the children and he said, Who are they?

Jacob answered, They are the children God has been pleased to give your servant.

And the maidservants and their children came forward and bowed down, and Leah and her children came forward and bowed down, and then Joseph and Rachel came and they bowed down.

Esau asked, What did you have in mind with all these herds I met on my way?

Jacob said, To find favor in your lordship's eyes!

Esau said, I have enough of my own, brother. Keep what is yours.

Jacob said, No, indeed! Show me your favor and accept these presents from my hands, because I have looked at your face as if it were the face of the Lord and you have been gracious to me. Accept these presents God has been so gracious as to give me! I have more than enough.

And Jacob urged him, and Esau accepted and said, Let us be on our way. I will go with you.

But Jacob said, My lord knows children are tender, and the ewes and cows are nursing their young. If I drive them too hard they will die. Go ahead, my lord, and let me move at my own pace and join my lord at Seir.

Esau said, Then let me leave some of my men to help you.

But Jacob said, Why, my lord? All I want is your gracious kindness. And so Esau returned to Seir, and Jacob pitched his tents at Succoth.

≈ ≈ ≈

DINAH, the daughter Leah had borne to Jacob, went out to visit among the women of the land. When Shechem, the son of Hamor the Hivite, the ruler of the country, saw Dinah, he took her by force and lay with her, and he became attached to Jacob's daughter and loved the girl and spoke tenderly to her. Shechem said to his father Hamor, Get me this girl to be my wife.

Jacob heard how he had defiled his daughter Dinah, but his sons were out in the fields with the cattle and Jacob said nothing until they came home.

Shechem's father, Hamor, came to Jacob to talk with him. Jacob's sons, who heard what had happened, had come in from the fields. The men were perturbed and very angry, because it was an outrage to Israel that Shechem had lain with Dinah, something that ought never to be done.

But Hamor said, My son Shechem loves your daughter. I ask you to give her to him to be his wife. Marry with us; give us your daughters and take our daughters in marriage. Settle among us; the land shall be open to you to live in, and trade in and acquire possessions.

And Shechem said to Dinah's father and to her brothers, Show me your kindness. Whatever the bride price, I will give it to you, only let me have the girl to be my wife.

But Jacob's sons answered Shechem and his father Hamor deceitfully because he had defiled their sister. They said to him, We cannot do that. To give our sister to a man who is not circumcised would be a disgrace among us. We will consent on condition that you become like us and have every man among you circumcised. Then we will give you our daughters in marriage and take your daughters to be our wives and settle among you, and we will become one people. If you don't do as we say and don't become circumcised, we'll take our daughters and be gone.

Hamor and his son Shechem were pleased with what they said. The young man lost no time in doing what they had asked, because he wanted Jacob's daughter, and he was the most respected man in his father's household.

Hamor and his son Shechem went to the town gates and spoke to their townsmen and said, These are peaceable men and mean well by us, therefore let them live in our land and trade in it. Look! The land is large enough. Let's take their daughters to be our wives and give them our daughters. They consent to live among us and be one people with us, but only if every one of our men is circumcised as they are circumcised. And wouldn't their flocks and all their wealth and every one of their animals be ours if we do what they say and they settle among us?

Everyone at the gate agreed with what Hamor and Shechem said to them and every man among them was circumcised.

It happened on the third day, when they were sore, that Dinah's two brothers, Simeon and Levi, took up their swords and fell upon the city and slew every male that was in it. They slew Hamor and Shechem and took Dinah from Shechem's house and they went away. The rest of Jacob's sons fell upon the slain men, and plundered the town where their sister had been defiled. They seized their flocks and their herds and their asses and everything in the town and everything out in the fields, all their wealth, and their little ones

and their wives and all that was in the houses they took as captive and booty.

And Jacob said to Simeon and Levi, You have brought down trouble upon me because you have put me in bad odor with the Canaanites and the Perizzites and all the people who live in this land. We are few in number. They will join forces against me and they will kill me, and I and all my household will be destroyed. But they said, Do you want our sister to be treated like a whore?

⁂ ⁂ ⁂

AND GOD SPOKE TO JACOB and said, Go to Bethel. Camp there and build an altar to the God who appeared to you when you were fleeing your brother Esau.

When they came to Bethel, Deborah, Rebekah's nurse, died and was buried under an oak.

And they left Bethel and were not far from Ephrath when Rachel began to give birth. It was a hard birth and as she labored the midwife said to her, Don't you worry! It is another son!

And Rachel's soul left her body—for she was dying—and she called the child Ben-oni, meaning son of suffering, but his father called him Benjamin, child of my right hand.

Rachel died and was buried on the road to Ephrath, which is called Bethlehem. And Jacob set up a pillar over her grave.

And Jacob, who was called Israel, had twelve sons and their names were Reuben, Simeon, Levi, Judah, Issachar, Zebulun, Dan, Naphtali, Gad, and Asher, and the two sons of Rachel, Joseph and Benjamin.

And Jacob came home to his father

Isaac at Hebron, and Isaac lived a hundred and eighty years and died, and his two sons Esau and Jacob buried him.

≈ ≈ ≈

AND JACOB SETTLED in the land of Canaan, the land where his father had been a stranger. And Joseph was a young boy of seventeen and tended the sheep with his brothers, the sons of his father's wives, and Joseph came to their father and told tales on them.

Jacob loved Joseph best because he was the child of his old age, and he made him a coat of many colors. The brothers saw that their father loved Joseph best and they hated him and never said a kind word to him.

And Joseph had a dream and told it to his brothers. He said, Listen to this dream that I have dreamed. We were binding sheaves of grain in the fields, and my sheaf stood up and remained standing, and your sheaves stood in a ring around my sheaf and bowed down before it.

His brothers said, You'd like to be a king, wouldn't you, and rule over us? And they hated him all the more, because of his dream.

And Joseph had another dream, and said, Come and hear another dream that I have dreamed. The sun, the moon, and eleven stars all bowed down before me.

He told his dream to his father, and his father became angry and said, What kind of a dream is that for you to be dreaming! Are we to come, your mother and I and all your brothers, and bow ourselves down to the ground before you?

His brothers were jealous, but his father kept these things in his mind.

One day he said to Joseph, Come! Your

brothers are grazing the flocks in the fields of Shechem. I want you to go and see how they are, and how the flocks are doing, and come back and tell me.

Joseph left and came to Shechem. And a certain man found him wandering in a field and asked him, What are you looking for?

He said, I'm looking for my brothers. Can you tell me where they have gone to graze their flocks?

The man said, I heard them talking. They said, Let's go on to Dothan.

Joseph followed his brothers to Dothan. They saw him coming from afar and made a plan how they might kill him. They said, Here comes the dreamer! Let's kill him and throw him in a pit in the ground. We'll say a wild animal devoured him; then we shall see what will become of his dreams.

Reuben heard what they were saying. He wanted to save Joseph from his brothers and said, Let us not kill him. Throw him in that pit and leave him in the wilderness. Let us shed no blood!— for he wanted to save him and bring him home to his father.

And it happened when Joseph came to his brothers that they tore his coat of many colors from his back and threw him in the pit—and it was dry. There was no water in the pit.

And so they sat down and ate their supper and raised their eyes and look! A caravan of Ishmaelites came with their camels loaded with precious spices, balsam, and myrrh, on their way down to Egypt.

Judah said, What good is it to kill the boy and cover up his blood? He is our brother—our own flesh. Let's sell him to the Ishmaelites and we'll not lay a hand on him.

The brothers agreed and when the Ishmaelites came by, they pulled Joseph out of the pit and sold him for twenty pieces of silver, and the merchants took Joseph down to Egypt with them.

Now Reuben came back and saw that Joseph was not in the pit, and tore his clothes, and went to his brothers and said, The child is gone! And I—what am I going to do?

And the brothers took Joseph's coat of many colors, slaughtered a goat and dipped the coat into the blood, and brought it to their father and said, Look what we have found. Do you know if this is your son's coat or not?

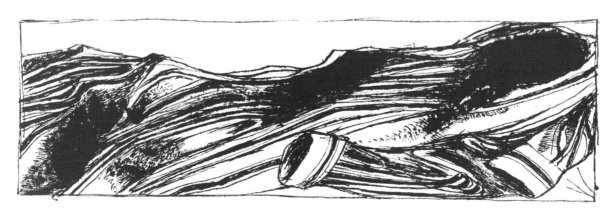

Jacob knew the coat of many colors and said, This is my son's coat! An evil beast has devoured him! Torn! Torn in pieces is my son! And Jacob tore his clothes and put on sackcloth and mourned his son. All his sons and daughters came to comfort him, but he would not be comforted and said, I will go down to my grave mourning for my son Joseph! That is how Joseph's father wept for him.

But the merchants took Joseph down to Egypt and sold him to Potiphar, one of Pharaoh's courtiers, the captain of his guard.

⚹ ⚹ ⚹

IT WAS ABOUT THIS TIME that Judah parted from his brothers to go and live near a certain Adullamite, whose name was Hirah. There Judah saw the daughter of a Canaanite called Shua, and took her to be his wife. Judah lay with her and she conceived and bore a son and he named him Er, and she conceived again and bore a son and named him Onan. And she conceived once more and bore another son and named him Shelah; and he was in Chezib when she bore him.

And Judah took a wife for his firstborn, Er. Her name was Tamar. Er did things that displeased the Lord and the Lord took his life. And Judah said to Onan, Take your brother's wife to be your wife; do your duty so that your seed will give your brother a child.

Onan knew that his seed would not count as his own and when he went in to lie with his brother's wife, he spilled his seed on the ground and let it spoil so that his seed should not give his brother a son.

What he did displeased the Lord, and He took Onan's life as well.

And Judah said to his daughter-in-law Tamar, Remain a widow and live in your father's house until my son Shelah has grown up. Judah thought that Shelah might die like his brothers. And so Tamar went to live in her father's house.

Time passed and Judah's wife died, and when Judah had finished mourning and felt comforted, he went up to see his sheep shearers, together with his friend Hirah, the Adullamite.

They told Tamar, Look, your father-in-law is going up to Timnah to his sheep shearing.

Tamar took off her widow's dress, covered her face with a veil, wrapped herself up, and sat by the gate of Enaim on the road to Timnah, because she knew Shelah had grown up and she had not been given to him to be his wife.

Judah saw her and thought she was a harlot, because she had covered her face. He turned off the road and went to her and said, Won't you let me come in and lie with you?—He didn't know she was his daughter-in-law—And she said, What will you pay me?

He said, I'll send you a goat from my flock. She said, You must leave me a pledge until you send it. He said, What pledge shall I leave you? She said, Your seal and cord and the staff you carry in your hands. And he gave them to her and came in and lay with her and she conceived.

And Tamar rose up and went on her way and took off her veil and put on her widow's dress again.

Judah sent his friend the Adullamite with the goat in order to redeem his pledge but he could not find the woman. He asked the townspeople, Where is the harlot who sat on the road by the gate of Enaim?—They said, There was no harlot here.

He went back to Judah and said, I couldn't find her, and the townspeople say there was no harlot here.

Judah said, Let her keep the things or we shall become a laughingstock. Look, I sent the goat, and you couldn't find her.

Three months passed and they told Judah, Your daughter-in-law, Tamar, has played the harlot and her whoring has gotten her with child. And Judah said, Have her brought out and let her be burned.

When Tamar was brought out she sent a message to her father-in-law saying, I am with child by the man to whom these things belong. And she said, Do you recognize this seal, the cord, and the staff?

Judah recognized them and said, There is more justice on her side than on mine, because I did not give her to my son Shelah. And he never lay with her again.

When the time came for her to give birth there were twins in her womb! While she was in labor it happened that one of them put his hand out. The midwife took a red thread and tied it around his hand and said, This one came out first. But it happened that he drew his hand back inside and out came his brother! She said, What a breach you have made for yourself! And they called him Perez, meaning he makes a breach.

After that his brother came out with the red thread around his hand, and they called him Zerah, meaning bright.

And the sons of Judah were Er, Onan, and Shelah, and Er and Onan died in Canaan. And the twin sons Tamar bore her father-in-law Judah were called Perez and Zerah.

⁊ ⁊ ⁊

AND THE LORD WAS WITH JOSEPH, and everything he did went well. He lived in the house of his Egyptian master, and Potiphar saw that the Lord was with Joseph, and Joseph prospered in everything he did. Potiphar liked Joseph and made Joseph his attendant and put Joseph in charge of all his household and of everything he owned, and from that day everything prospered. The Lord blessed everything the Egyptian owned at home and in the field, for Joseph's sake. And the Egyptian left everything in Joseph's care, and he himself did nothing but eat and drink.

Now Joseph was a beautiful young man and well built, and his master's wife looked at him and said, Come, lie with me.

But Joseph would not and said, You know my master has put all his household and everything he owns into my hands. He himself is no greater in his own house than he has made me. He denies me nothing except you, because you are his wife. How could I sin against God and do such a wicked thing!

Day in and day out she urged Joseph to be with her and lie with her, but he would not.

It happened, one day, that he went into

the house to see to his work, and there were no servants in the room. Potiphar's wife took hold of Joseph's coat and said, Lie with me. But Joseph left his coat in her hand and ran out of the house, and she screamed for the servants and said, You see what this Hebrew my husband has brought into the house has done! He makes nothing but trouble! He came in here and wanted to lie with me, but I screamed and he ran out of the house. This is his coat!

When her husband came home she told him the same story and said, You see what that Hebrew slave you brought into this house has done to me!

Potiphar burned with anger and took

Joseph and threw him into the prison house where they put Pharaoh's prisoners, and Joseph remained there in prison.

But the Lord was with Joseph, and the warden of the prison liked him and put him in charge of all the prisoners. Anything that needed to be done in the prison had to be done through Joseph. Now that the warden had Joseph to do everything, he needed to do nothing at all. And the Lord was with Joseph and everything he did prospered.

∝ ∝ ∝

AFTER A TIME it happened that Pharaoh's chief cupbearer and his chief baker offended their master. Pharaoh was angry

with them and had them thrown in the same prison, and the warden gave them Joseph to be their attendant.

And so they were in the prison for a time, and Pharaoh's cupbearer and Pharaoh's baker each dreamed a dream, in the same night, and each dream had its own meaning.

In the morning Joseph came in and said, Why do you look sad?

They said, We have each had a dream and there is no one here to interpret our dreams for us.

Joseph said, Only God interprets. Tell me your dreams.

The chief cupbearer told Joseph his dream. He said, I dreamed I saw a vine that had three branches and put out leaves and blossomed, and the grapes ripened. I had Pharaoh's cup in my hand and I took the grapes and pressed them out into Pharaoh's cup and put the cup into Pharaoh's hand.

Joseph said, This is the interpretation. The three branches are three days. In three days Pharaoh will send for you and give you back your post, and you will put his cup into his hand as you used to do, when you were his cupbearer. Remember me in your good fortune! Speak to Pharaoh about me and get me out of this prison. I was brought by force out of the land of the Hebrews, nor have I done anything here for which I deserve to be thrown in prison.

Now when the chief baker saw that Joseph's interpretation promised the cupbearer a good fortune, he said, I had a dream too. I dreamed that I carried three baskets of white bread on my head and in

the topmost basket was every sort of fine baked goods for Pharaoh, and the birds ate them out of the basket on the top of my head.

Joseph said, This is the interpretation of your dream: The three baskets are three days. In three days Pharaoh will send for you and hang you on a tree, and the birds will eat your flesh from your bones.

It happened that the third day was Pharaoh's birthday. He had a feast for all his court and sent for the chief cupbearer and the chief baker and gave the chief cupbearer back his post, and the cupbearer put the cup into Pharaoh's hand as he used to do. The chief baker he hanged on a tree and everything happened as Joseph said. But the chief cupbearer did not think of Joseph and forgot about him.

⁂ ⁂ ⁂

TWO YEARS PASSED and Pharaoh dreamed that he stood by the Nile and saw seven fine, fat cows come out of the water and graze among the reeds on the meadow. Then seven more cows came out of the water, but they were ugly and thin and they went to stand beside the fine, fat cows on the banks of the Nile. And the ugly, thin cows swallowed up the seven fine, fat cows. And Pharaoh woke.

He fell asleep again, and again he dreamed and saw seven ears of grain, healthy and full, growing out of one stalk. Then there sprouted seven ears of grain that were thin and scorched by the east wind. The thin ears of grain swallowed up the healthy, full ears. And Pharaoh woke, and knew it was a dream.

When morning came he was troubled. He sent for his magicians and all the wise men of Egypt and told them his dreams, but there was not one who could interpret his dreams for him.

Now the chief cupbearer said, This is the day to put me in mind of my sins! That time when Pharaoh was angry with his servants, and threw me and the chief baker in prison, we each had a dream in

the very same night. There was a young Hebrew in the prison with us. He interpreted our dreams and each dream meant something different and everything turned out as he had said: I was returned to my post, and the other was hanged.

And Pharaoh sent for Joseph, and Joseph was quickly brought out of the prison. They cut his hair and changed his clothes and brought him before Pharaoh.

Pharaoh said, I have had a dream, and there is no one who can interpret it. They tell me that you know how to interpret dreams.

Joseph said, It is not up to me, but God, who will show Pharaoh His favor.

Pharaoh said, I dreamed that I stood by the Nile and saw seven fine, fat cows come out of the water and graze among the reeds in the meadow. Then I saw seven more cows and they were skinny and lean and ugly, and they came out of the water; nowhere in all of Egypt have I ever seen such ugly cows. And the seven lean, ugly cows swallowed up the first seven fine, fat cows and no one would have known that they had eaten them, they were as ugly and skinny as ever. Then I woke.

Again I slept and had another dream. I saw seven ears of grain, healthy and full, growing out of one stalk. Then there sprouted seven ears of grain that were thin and scorched by the east wind, and the seven thin ears swallowed up the full ears. I have told my wise men and they don't know what it means.

Joseph said, Pharaoh's two dreams mean the same thing. God has made known to Pharaoh what is to come. The seven fine cows mean seven years, and the seven good ears of grain mean the same seven years of abundance; it is one and the same dream. The seven ugly, lean cows that step out of the water are seven years, and the seven thin, scorched ears of corn are the same seven years of famine. There will be seven abundant years throughout the land of Egypt, followed by seven years of famine, and the seven years of famine will ravage the land so that no one will remember the seven abundant years. Hunger will be so great that the abundance will be forgotten. Because Pharaoh has dreamed the same dream twice it means that God is sure to do all this and soon.

And Joseph said, Now let Pharaoh find a man who is wise and capable and put him in charge of the land of Egypt. Let him make sure that there shall be governors in every part of the land who will take a fifth part of the harvest of the seven abundant years and store the grain in Pharaoh's storehouses for the use of the cities during the seven years of famine that will come upon Egypt, or the country will be ravaged by hunger.

The plan seemed good to Pharaoh and to his court and Pharaoh said, Where shall we find another man in whom the spirit of God speaks as He speaks in this man? Because God has made all these things known to you, there is no one so full of understanding and wisdom as you. You shall have charge over my palace, and all my people shall obey you. Only inasmuch as I sit on the throne shall I be greater than you.

Pharaoh took the ring from his finger

and put it on Joseph's finger. He gave him robes of precious linen and put a golden chain around his neck and made him ride in the chariot of his second in command, and they ran ahead of Joseph crying, Bow down, for Pharaoh has put Egypt under the charge of this man!

And Pharaoh said to Joseph, I am Pharaoh, but without you no one lifts a hand or a foot in all the land of Egypt.

And Pharaoh gave Joseph Asenath, the daughter of the priest of On, to be his wife. Joseph was thirty years old when he entered the service of Pharaoh, king of Egypt. And Joseph left Pharaoh's court and traveled through all the land.

For seven abundant years the land produced plentifully. Joseph collected the harvests of those seven years and stored them. In each city he stored the food that grew in the fields round about. Joseph heaped up such a quantity of grain he had to stop keeping count, for the quantity was measureless as the sands of the sea.

Asenath bore Joseph two sons. Joseph called his firstborn Manasseh, meaning God makes me forget the griefs I suffered in the house of my father. The second son he named Ephraim, meaning God makes me prosper in the land of my hardships.

The seven abundant years came to an end in Egypt, and the seven years of famine began, as Joseph had foretold. And there was famine in all the lands round about. Only in Egypt was there bread to eat. When the Egyptians were hungry and came to Pharaoh crying for bread, Pharaoh said, Go to Joseph and do what he says.

And now Joseph opened the storehouses and sold the grain to the Egyptians, and the longer the famine lasted the more severe it became, and the whole world came to Egypt to buy grain from Joseph, for the famine was terrible everywhere.

⁂

NOW WHEN JACOB HEARD that there was grain to be had in Egypt, he said to his sons, Why do you stand there looking at one another? Go down to Egypt and buy us some grain so that we can live and not die.

He did not send Joseph's little brother Benjamin with them, because he was afraid of what might happen to him.

The famine was severe in Canaan. Jacob's sons were among many people traveling down to Egypt. Joseph sold grain to everyone who came, and Joseph's brothers came and stood before him and bowed their faces to the ground. Joseph knew they were his brothers and remembered the dreams that he had dreamed, but he acted as if they were strangers and spoke roughly to them and said, Where are you from?

They said, We have come from Canaan to buy grain. They didn't know it was Joseph.

Joseph said, Spies—that's what you are! You've come to spy out the weakness of this land!

They answered, No, my lord! We are your lordship's servants and have come to buy grain. We are brothers, the sons of one man, and honest men. We are not spies!

Joseph said, No! The weakness of the land is what you've come to spy out.

They said, My lord, there are twelve of us, sons of one man, who lives in Canaan. The youngest is home with his father, and there was another brother, but he's no longer here.

Joseph said, And I say you're spies! I will put you to the test. One of you go home and get this youngest brother about whom you have told me. Bring him here. The rest of you can wait in prison. As Pharaoh lives, you're not leaving here unless you bring me your youngest brother and I see that the story you have told me is the truth. If not, as Pharaoh lives, you're spies and you shall die! And he put all of them in prison for three days.

On the third day Joseph said to them, Do what I say and no harm shall come to you. I am a God-fearing man. Prove to me that you are honest men. Leave one of your brothers here in prison. The rest of you go home. Take back the grain you have bought to feed your hungry families and bring me your youngest brother. Then I'll believe the story you have told me. If not you shall die.

And they complied, but they said, one to the other, Our guilt has found us out because of Joseph. We saw his soul's anguish when he pleaded with us, and we would not listen! That's why this misery has come upon us!

Reuben said, Didn't I tell you not to harm the child? You wouldn't listen to me. Now we are paying for his blood.

They did not know that Joseph understood what they were saying, because he spoke with them through an interpreter, and Joseph turned away from them and wept. Then he turned back, and he took Simeon and had him bound before their eyes.

Now Joseph ordered their bags to be filled with grain and had each man's money put back into the mouth of his bag. Joseph's brothers loaded their bags onto their asses and went on their way.

Now when they stopped for the night, one of them opened his bag to feed his ass and there was his money, lying in the mouth of his bag! He said, My money has got back into my bag!

Their hearts sank. They trembled and

looked at one another and said, What is God doing to us!

They came home to their father Jacob, in Canaan, and told him what had happened. They said, The man who is the lord of Egypt spoke harshly to us and thought that we were spies. We said, We are not spies! We are honest men, twelve brothers, the sons of one father. One brother is no longer here, and the youngest is home with his father. But the man said, Prove to me that you are honest men. Leave one of your brothers here, take back as much grain as you need for your households and go home, but bring me back your youngest brother. Then I shall know you are not spies but honest men, and I'll give you back your brother and you'll be free to trade in Egypt.

And now they opened their bags and each one found his purse full of his money in the mouth of his bag and they were frightened, and Jacob was frightened. He said, You rob me of one child after another! Joseph is no longer here and Simeon is no longer here and now you want to take Benjamin. Everything goes against me!

Reuben said, Put Benjamin under my care. If I don't bring the boy back, you can put my two sons to death! I pledge myself for him.

But Jacob said, My son is not going to Egypt with you. His brother is dead and he is the only one left—if something happened to him on the way it would bring my gray head down to the grave with sorrow.

≈ ≈ ≈

BUT THE FAMINE WAS BITTER in Canaan, and when they had eaten up the grain from Egypt, their father said, Go back and buy more food.

Now Judah said, The man made it clear he will not see us unless our brother comes with us. If you let Benjamin come, we will go down and buy you some food to eat. If you don't let him go we won't go back, because the man will not see us.

Jacob said, You did me an evil turn when you told the man you had another brother! Why did you tell him?

They said, Because he questioned us and asked us about ourselves and our family. He asked us, Is your father still alive? How many brothers are you? We answered his questions. How could we know he would say, Bring your brother back with you.

Judah said, Let the boy go with me, in my care, so that we can go and get food for you and for us and for our little ones, so that we can live and not die. I pledge myself for the boy. If I don't bring him back and set him here before you, the guilt be upon my head my life long. We've waited so long we could have gone and returned twice over.

Their father said, If it must be so, then take with you the best fruits of this land and bring the man gifts—a little balsam and some honey, spices and myrrh, nuts and almonds. Take money, and take back the money you found in your bags. Perhaps there was some mistake. Yes, and take your brother. Go back to the man. May God Almighty make him merciful to you and give you back your brother

Simeon and let you bring Benjamin back! As for me, if I must lose my child I must lose him!

And so they took the gifts and twice the sums of money and they took Benjamin with them and set out for Egypt. And they came and stood before Joseph, and Joseph saw they had brought Benjamin with them and he said to his steward, Take them to my house. Slaughter an animal and cook it. These men will eat their midday meal with me.

The steward did as Joseph said, but the men were afraid and said, one to the other, It's because of the money we found in our bags last time. That's why they're taking us to his house—so they can fall on us and make us their slaves and take our asses!

They stopped the steward at the entrance of the house and said, Sir, if you please, we came down once before, to buy grain, and when we stopped for the night, and opened our bags, each of us found his money, in the exact weight, right in the mouth of his bag, and so we have brought it back with us. And we have brought more money to buy grain. We don't know how the money got back into your bags.

The man said, It's all right. Don't worry. Your God, and the God of your father, put your purses back into your bags. I received your payment in full.

And he brought Simeon out to them and took them into the house and gave them water to bathe their feet and fodder for their asses. And they made their presents ready, for they had heard they were to eat their midday meal in Joseph's house.

Joseph entered the room and they gave him their presents and bowed down to the ground before him. He greeted them and said, And how is the old man, your father about whom you told me? Is he still alive?

They said, Our father is alive and is well, your lordship. And they bowed down to the ground. Joseph looked at his brother Benjamin, his own mother's son, and said, So this is the youngest brother about whom you told me? May the Lord be merciful to you, my son.

And Joseph said nothing more and hurried from the room. His heart yearned with love for his younger brother, and he looked for a place where he could weep and went into his chamber and wept and then he washed his face and returned to them and, keeping his feelings in check, said, You may serve the meal.

They served him, where he sat by himself, and the Egyptians ate by themselves, because it was an abomination to the Egyptians to eat at the same table with Hebrews. But Joseph's brothers they seated in the order of their birth, from the firstborn to the youngest, so that they looked at one another in astonishment. They were served from Joseph's own table, and Benjamin's portion was five times as large as any of the others' and they ate and drank in good spirits.

Now Joseph instructed his steward and said, Fill each man's bag with as much grain as he can carry, and put each man's full purse back into the mouth of his bag. Put my silver cup in the mouth of the bag of the youngest, along with his grain and his money. And the man did what Joseph said. In the morning when it became light they sent the brothers off with their asses, and they left the city.

They had not gone far when Joseph said to his steward, Go after those men. When you catch up with them, say, Why do you repay kindness with evil? Why have you taken my master's silver cup out of which he drinks and which he uses for divinations? What a wicked thing to do!

And the steward pursued Joseph's brothers and caught up with them and repeated Joseph's words to them. They said, Why does your lordship say such things to us? We would never do such a thing! Didn't we bring back the money we found in our bags? Why would we steal your lord's silver and gold out of his house? If you find it on any one of us, that one shall die, and the rest of us will be your lordship's slaves!

He said, Very well, but only he in whose bag the thing is found shall be my slave; the rest of you will be free to go.

Each one quickly lowered his bag to the ground and opened his bag, and the steward made his search beginning with the eldest and ending with the youngest, and he found the cup in Benjamin's bag.

And now they tore their clothes, reloaded their asses, and so they came back to the city.

The steward took them to Joseph's house, and they threw themselves down before him with their faces to the ground.

Joseph said, How could you do such a thing? Don't you know I am a man who divines the truth?

Judah said, My lord, what can we say? How can we prove our innocence? God has found out your servants' crime. We and the boy in whose sack the cup was found are your lordship's slaves.

Joseph said, I would not be so unjust. Only he who had my cup shall be my slave. The rest of you go home to your father.

Now Judah stepped before him. He said, My lord, allow your servant to speak a word in your lordship's ear, and do not be angry with your servant, you, who have the greatness of Pharaoh himself! The first time your servants came before your lordship, you questioned us and asked us if we had a father and brothers. We told your lordship we had a father and that he was old, and that we had a little brother born to my father's old age, and another brother who is dead, and only this one boy is left of his mother's sons, and his father loves him. Your lordship said to your servants, Bring me the boy, and I will be gracious to him! We told your lordship, If the boy leaves his father, his father will die! But your lordship said, Unless your brother comes with you, you shall not see my face! We went home to our father and told him your lordship's words. Our father said, Go back and buy us some more food! But we said, We cannot go. The man will not see us unless our youngest brother comes with us! Our father said, You know my wife bore me two sons in my old age. One is gone and I told myself an animal has torn my son—torn him to pieces—and I never saw his face again! Now you want to take this child away from me! And so I pledged myself to our father for the boy's safety and said, If I don't bring the boy back to you, I shall bear the guilt my life long! Therefore let me remain and be your lordship's slave in the boy's stead. Let the child go home with his brothers, for how can I go home and witness my father's sorrow and bear to see grief bring his gray head down to the grave?

Now Joseph could not control himself any longer in front of all his servants and cried, Get everybody out of here! And so no one was by when Joseph made himself known to his brothers and wept so loudly the Egyptians could hear him and Pharaoh's household was told of it.

Joseph said, I am Joseph! Is my father still alive?

The brothers could not answer, they were so horrified in his presence. But Joseph said, Won't you come closer to me?

And they came closer, and he said, I am Joseph, your brother, whom you sold into Egypt! Don't grieve, and don't be frightened of my anger because you sold me here, to this place. It was God who sent me ahead to save your lives. The famine has lasted two years, and it will be another five years before there will be any plowing or reaping. God sent me to

prepare a great salvation for you and your children and your children's children on the earth. It was not you, it was the Lord, who sent me here to be a father to Pharaoh and a steward of his household, and to govern all the land of Egypt. Hurry home to my father and say, Your son Joseph says, God has made me lord over the land of Egypt. Come to me! Hurry! You shall live in the land of Goshen where I can be near you and can provide for you and your children and your children's children, your flocks and herds and all you have, because there are five years of famine yet to come. And he said to them, It is true! It is me! It is me your eyes, and my brother Benjamin's eyes, are seeing! It is my mouth speaking to you. Go tell my father and bring him to me. Hurry!

And he threw his arms around his brother Benjamin and wept, and Benjamin wept on his brother Joseph's neck. And Joseph kissed all his brothers and wept with them, and now his brothers could talk with him.

The news reached Pharaoh's palace: Joseph's brothers have come to Egypt! And it pleased Pharaoh and his court. Pharaoh said, Tell your brothers, all that is best in Egypt shall be theirs; they shall live on the fat of the land! And Joseph gave each of his brothers a splendid robe, but to Benjamin he gave three hundred silver pieces and five robes. And for his father he sent ten asses loaded with the best things of Egypt, and ten she-asses loaded with grain. To his brothers he said, You are not to quarrel among yourselves along the way!

And they left Egypt and came home to their father in Canaan and told him, Joseph is alive! He is the man who rules over all the land of Egypt.

But Jacob's heart was numb; he did not believe them. They told him everything Joseph had said to them, and when he saw the carriages sent to carry him to Egypt, Jacob's spirit lifted. And they went down to Egypt, Jacob and his children and his children's children. There were in all seventy persons in Jacob's household, who went to Egypt with him.

And Joseph put horses to his carriage and came out to meet his father, and when he saw him he threw his arms around his father and wept long upon his neck.

And Jacob said, Now I can die, for I have seen your face again and know that you are alive!

≈ ≈ ≈

JACOB, WHOM THE LORD HAD NAMED Israel, lived in Egypt and settled in the land of Goshen and grew and multiplied. He lived in Egypt for seventeen years and was one hundred and forty-seven years old.

Now the time came for him to die, and he called for his son Joseph and said, If you have a kindness for me, do not bury me in Egypt! Lay your hand under my thigh and swear you will keep faith with me and will carry me out of Egypt and lay me in the grave where my fathers lie buried.

Joseph said, I myself will do what you ask.

But Jacob said, Swear it!

And Joseph swore it, and Israel bowed down at the head of his bed.

Time passed and they came and told Joseph, Your father is ill!

Joseph took with him his two sons Manasseh and Ephraim. They said to Jacob, Look, your son Joseph has come to see you! Israel gathered all his strength and sat up in his bed and saw Joseph's sons and asked, Who are they?—for Israel's eyes were dim with age and he could not see.

Joseph said, They are the sons whom God has given me in Egypt.

Israel said, Bring them here so that I may bless them.

And Joseph brought them to Israel, and he kissed them and embraced them and said, I did not think that I would ever see your face again, and now God has let me see your children too!

Joseph took the boys from his father's lap and bowed down with his face to the ground and with his right hand he took Ephraim and made him stand by Israel's left hand and took Manasseh with his left hand and made him stand at his father's right hand, and brought them close to his father. But Israel reached out his right hand and laid it on the head of Ephraim, the younger, and crossed his arms and laid his left hand on Manasseh's head, though he was the firstborn.

Joseph saw what his father did and did not like it and took his father's hand and moved it to Manasseh's head, and said, No, my father, this one is the firstborn. Put your right hand on his head. But his father would not and said, I know, my son, I know! He, too, will become a nation, and become great. But his younger brother will become greater and will be a community of nations. And he blessed them and put Ephraim, the younger, ahead of Manasseh, the firstborn.

And Israel said, Look, I am dying! God will be with you and will bring you back to the land of your fathers.

And Jacob blessed his twelve sons, the twelve tribes of Israel, and said, Now I am going to my people. Do not bury me in Egypt, I beg you, but bury me with my fathers in the cave in the field in Canaan, where they buried Abraham and his wife Sarah, where they buried Isaac and his wife Rebekah, where I buried Leah! My Rachel died on the way back to Canaan, not far from Ephrath—which they call Bethlehem—and I buried her there, beside the road!

When Jacob had finished speaking he drew his feet up on the bed, and died, and was gathered to his people.

Joseph threw himself upon his father and wept over him and kissed him. And Joseph commanded the physicians who were in his service to embalm his father Israel, and the physicians embalmed him, and took the full forty days that is the time required for embalming. And the Egyptians mourned him for seventy days.

When the days of mourning had passed, Joseph went to Pharaoh's court and said, If I have your favor, speak for me to Pharaoh. Tell him my father made me swear an oath to him saying, Look, I am dying. You must bury me in the tomb which I dug for myself in the land of Canaan. Therefore let me go and bury my father and then I will return.

Pharaoh said, Go and bury your father, as he made you swear to do.

And Joseph went to bury his father. And there went with him the officers of Pharaoh's court and the elders of Egypt, and the members of Joseph's household and his brothers and everyone belonging to his father's household. Only the children and the flocks and herds were left behind in Goshen. And the chariots went with them and the horsemen—a very large company.

When they came to the threshing floor of Atad, near the Jordan, Joseph observed the seven days of mourning for his father and mourned with a great and bitter lamentation, and the Canaanites who lived near the threshing floor of Atad saw them and said, Look at the Egyptians mourning!

And Jacob's sons did as their father had commanded them and carried him to the land of Canaan and buried him in the cave in the field of Machpelah near Mamre, which Abraham had bought as a burial place from Ephron the Hittite. And after he had buried his father, Joseph returned to Egypt with his brothers and all the others who had gone to bury his father with him.

When Joseph's brothers saw that their

father was dead, they said, What if Joseph holds a grudge against us and pays us back—pays us back for all the wrongs we did him? And they sent to Joseph to say, Your father left word for you before he died. This is what he told us to say to you: Oh, forgive your brothers the wicked wrongs they have done you!

Joseph wept when they said this to him. And now his brothers came and threw themselves down before him and said, We have come to be your slaves!

Joseph said, Don't be afraid! Am I your God? It is true that you planned to harm me, but God turned the plan to good, to keep a great people alive! Now don't be afraid. I will provide for you and for your children! And he spoke kindly and comforted them.

And Joseph lived in Egypt with all his father's family, and he lived one hundred and ten years. He lived to see the third generation of Ephraim's children, and the children of Machir, Manasseh's son, grew up at Joseph's knee.

Then Joseph said to his brothers, I am dying. Surely God will come to you and take you out of this land and bring you into the land He swore to give to Abraham, Isaac, and Jacob. And Joseph made the sons of Israel swear to him saying, Surely God will come to you and when you leave this place you must carry my bones with you.

And Joseph died, and he was one hundred and ten years old, and they embalmed him, and laid him in a coffin in Egypt.

And the sons of Israel, who had come to Egypt with Jacob, were Reuben, Simeon, Levi, Judah, Issachar, Zebulun, Benjamin, Dan, Naphtali, Gad, and Asher, each with his household, seventy souls in all, and Joseph was already in Egypt.

≈ ≈ ≈

NOW JOSEPH HAD DIED, and all his brothers, and all the people who lived in those days, and the children of Israel grew and bore children, were fruitful and multiplied and became exceedingly strong, and the land was filled with them.

There was a new Pharaoh in Egypt who did not know about Joseph. He said to his people, Look at the children of Israel! They are too many against us; they are too strong. We must think what to do about them. What if war breaks out and they join our enemies? And what if they leave the country?

And Pharaoh oppressed the children of Israel and set slave masters over them who forced them to make bricks and build Pharaoh the cities of Pithom and Rameses. But the more the Egyptians abused the children of Israel the more they multiplied. They swarmed over the land, and the Egyptians came to abhor them and made their lives bitter and forced them to build with bricks and work the fields and had no pity on them.

And Pharaoh sent for the two Hebrew midwives Shiphrah and Puah and said, When you help a Hebrew woman to give birth, keep your eye on the child. If it's a boy, kill him; if it's a girl, let her live.

But the midwives were God-fearing women and did not do what Pharaoh said and let the boys live.

Pharaoh sent for them and said, What are you up to? Why are you letting the boys live!

The midwives answered, Hebrew women are not like the Egyptians. They are strong and lively and give birth before the midwives can get there!

And God blessed the two midwives and gave them children of their own. And the children of Israel multiplied and became many. And Pharaoh issued a proclamation to all his people: Throw every newborn boy into the Nile, but let the girls live.

≈ ≈ ≈

THERE WAS A MAN of the family of Levi who married a Levite girl. She conceived and bore a son and she saw that it was a fine boy. For three months she hid the baby and when she could no longer hide

him, she made a basket of rushes, coated it with tar and pitch, and laid the boy inside. She put the basket among the reeds on the bank of the Nile, and his sister stood a little way off to see what would happen.

And Pharaoh's daughter and her attendants came to bathe in the Nile and walked up and down the bank. She saw the basket in the reeds and sent her slave girl to bring it to her, and opened it—and look! Inside was a baby, and it was crying! She was sorry for the little boy and said, It's one of the Hebrew children.

Now his sister said, Shall I go and get one of the Hebrew women to nurse the child for you?

Pharaoh's daughter said, Yes. Go and find me one! And the girl went to fetch the baby's mother.

Pharaoh's daughter said, Take this little baby and nurse him for me. I will pay you.

And the woman took the baby and nursed him. When the child was old enough, she brought him to Pharaoh's daughter and he grew up in Pharaoh's court as her son. She named him Moses, meaning I drew him out of the water.

≈ ≈ ≈

TIME PASSED and Moses was grown and went out and watched his Hebrew brothers at their forced labor. Moses saw an Egyptian beating one of the Hebrews and he looked this way and that, and there was no one about and Moses struck down the Egyptian and buried him in the sand. Moses went out the next day and saw two Hebrews fighting. He spoke to the one who was in the wrong and said, Why are you fighting with your fellow Hebrew?

The man said, Who has appointed you to be our master and to judge us? Are you going to kill me, too, the way you killed the Egyptian?

Now Moses was afraid and thought, Everybody knows!

Pharaoh heard and wanted Moses killed, and Moses fled and came to the land of Midian, and sat down by a well.

There lived a priest in Midian who had seven daughters, and they came to fill the troughs and water their father's flock. Some shepherds came and chased them away, but Moses rose and helped them and drew water for them and watered their flocks.

The girls returned to their father, and he said, You are back early today!

They said, There was an Egyptian and he saved us from the shepherds. He even drew water for us and watered the flocks.

He said, Where is he? Why didn't you bring him in? Go and invite him to eat with us.

Moses agreed to stay with the man, and he gave Moses his daughter Zipporah in marriage. Zipporah bore Moses a son, and Moses named the child Gershom, meaning I was a stranger in a strange land.

A long time passed and Pharaoh died. Still the children of Israel groaned in their cruel bondage and cried aloud, and their cry rose to God. God heard their moans and the Lord remembered His covenant with Abraham and Isaac and Jacob, and God saw the children of Israel and kept them in His mind.

≈ ≈ ≈

MOSES TENDED THE FLOCKS of his father-in-law Jethro, the Midianite priest, and he led the flocks into the wilderness and came to the mountain of God.

And the angel of the Lord appeared to Moses in a fire burning in a bush of thorns. Moses looked and the bush burned and was not burned up!

Moses said, I'll go over and take a look at this wonderful sight—a burning bush that does not burn up!

The Lord saw Moses coming to look, and God called to him out of the bush and said, Moses, Moses!

Moses said, Here I am.

God said, Come no closer. Take your shoes off your feet. The place on which you stand is holy ground! And God said,

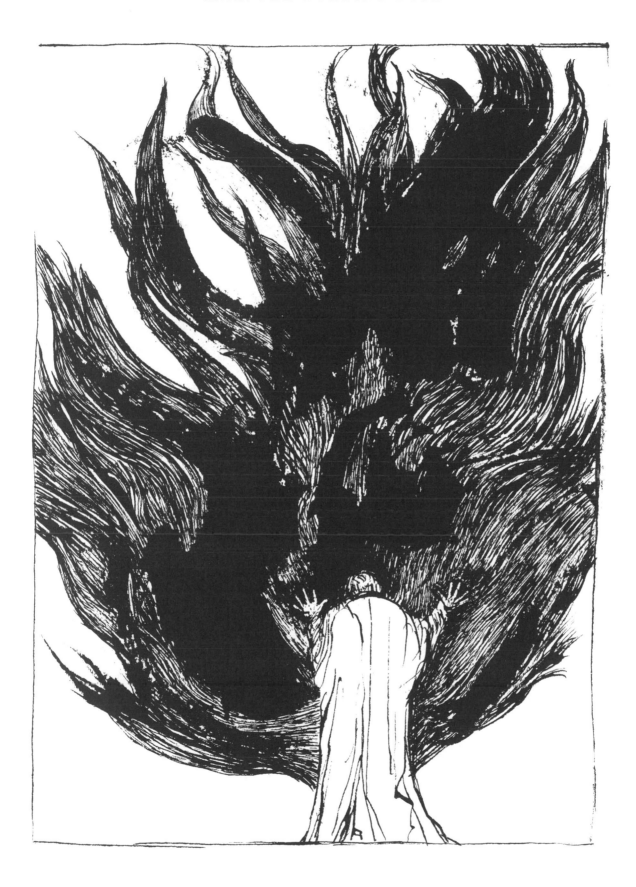

I am the God of your father, the God of Abraham, the God of Isaac, and the God of Jacob.

Moses hid his face, for he was afraid to look at God.

God said, I have seen—oh! I have seen—the misery of my people in Egypt! I have heard them cry aloud under the oppression of the slave drivers. I know their suffering. I have come down to snatch them out of the hand of the Egyptians. I shall lead them out of the land of Egypt into a good land, a wide land, a land flowing with milk and honey —the land of the Canaanites, the Hittites, the Amorites, the Perizzites, the Hivites, and the Jebusites. Go back to Egypt. I shall send you to speak to Pharaoh, and you will lead My people Israel out of Egypt.

But Moses said, Who am I, that I should

speak to Pharaoh? How can I lead Israel out of Egypt?

God said, I shall be with you and this will be a sign to you that it is I who have sent you. You will lead the people out of Egypt and on this mountain shall you worship God.

But Moses said, What if I go to the children of Israel and say to them: The God of your fathers has sent me to you! —and they ask me, What God? What is His name?—What shall I say to them?

God said, I AM THAT I AM. Say to the children of Israel, I AM has sent me to you. And God went on and said, This is what you shall say to them: He who has sent me is the Lord, the God of your fathers, the God of Abraham, the God of Isaac, and the God of Jacob. That is My name for ever and ever by which you and your children and your children's children shall call to Me. Now go and summon the elders of Israel and tell them what I have said to you. They will listen to you, and you will go to Pharaoh and say, The Lord, God of the Hebrews, has appeared to us and has spoken to us. Let us go on a three-day journey into the wilderness and sacrifice to the Lord our God. I know that Pharaoh will not let you go until a mighty hand has forced him. I shall stretch out the might of My hand and strike the Egyptians with all the wonders that I shall perform, and then he will let you go!

Moses said, What if they don't believe me and say, The Lord never appeared to you!

The Lord said, What is that in your hand?

Moses said, My staff.

The Lord said, Throw it on the ground.

Moses threw it on the ground, and it became a snake. Moses ran away, but the Lord said, Stretch out your hand. Catch it by the tail.

Moses stretched out his hand and caught hold, and it became a staff in his hand.

The Lord said, That is so they will believe it was the Lord, the God of their fathers, the God of Abraham, the God of Isaac, and the God of Jacob, who appeared to you. Then the Lord said, Come, put your hand inside your coat.

Moses put his hand inside his coat and when he drew it out the hand was leprous, as if encrusted with snow.

God said, Put your hand back in your coat.

Moses put his hand back in his coat and drew it out and his hand was healthy, like all his flesh!

The Lord said, If they do not believe the first sign, they will believe the second, and if they believe neither and will not listen, take water out of the Nile and spill it on the dry ground, and the water you shall take out of the Nile will turn to blood on the dry ground.

But Moses said, Ah, Lord, I am a man who doesn't speak easily—I never did, not as a child, nor as a man, not even now when my Lord is speaking to His servant. I am slow of speech; my tongue is heavy in my mouth.

The Lord said, Who gives man a mouth? Who makes a man deaf or dumb or seeing or blind? Is it not I, the Lord?

Now, go! I will be with your mouth and teach you what to say.

But Moses said, Lord, choose anyone You want except me!

Now the Lord became angry with Moses, and He said, I know your brother Aaron is a Levite, and a man who knows how to speak. He is already on his way to meet you. He will be happy to see you. I shall tell you what to say and you will put the words into Aaron's mouth. He will speak to the children of Israel for you as if he were your tongue and you will be as if you were his God. Now take your staff in your hand so you can perform signs and wonders. And God said to Moses, Go back to Egypt. All of those who wanted to kill you are dead.

Moses went to his father-in-law Jethro and said, Let me go back to my people in Egypt and see if they are alive.

Jethro said, Go in peace.

Moses took his wife and his two sons, put them on an ass, and took the staff of God in his hand.

᷾   ᷾   ᷾

AND THE LORD SPOKE TO AARON and said, Come, rise and go to meet your brother Moses in the wilderness.

Aaron went into the wilderness and met Moses by the mountain of God and Aaron kissed Moses, and Moses told Aaron everything the Lord had sent him to say, and the signs and wonders He had commanded him to perform. They called together the elders of the children of Israel, and Aaron told them everything that the Lord told Moses, and Moses performed the signs and wonders, and when the children of Israel learned that the Lord remembered them and thought of them, they bowed down and worshipped Him.

And Moses and Aaron went to Pharaoh and stood before him and said, The Lord, God of Israel, says, Let My people go into the wilderness and make Me a festival.

Pharaoh said, Who is this Lord and why should I do what He says? Why should I let Israel go? I don't know anything about this Lord and I will not let Israel go.

They said, He is the Lord, the God of the Hebrews, who has appeared to us, therefore let us make a three-day journey into the wilderness so that we can sacrifice to the Lord God, or He might send down a plague upon us or kill us with the sword.

But Pharaoh said, You, Moses and Aaron, want to take the people away from their duties. Go! Get back to your work. Look how many of you there are, and now you don't want to work!

On that same day Pharaoh summoned his slave drivers and said, From this day on don't give them straw to make the bricks. Let them collect their own straw, but make sure they make the same number of bricks they made yesterday. Don't let them get away with less. Lazy, that's what they are! That's why they say, Let us go into the wilderness so we can sacrifice to our God! Lean harder on them and they won't have time to listen to these lies.

The slave drivers went out and said, Pharaoh says, From now on I will not give you straw. Go gather your own straw.

And so the children of Israel had to go all over Egypt to gather the stubble to make straw for the bricks, and the slave drivers drove them and said, Make as many bricks as you made yesterday and no fewer! And they beat the Hebrew foremen and said, Why haven't you made your daily quota of bricks that you have always made before?

The Hebrew foremen went to Pharaoh and cried, What are you doing? It's your own people who won't give us the straw to make the bricks, and then they tell us to make our daily quota and beat us, when it's the fault of your own people!

Pharaoh said, Lazy, that's what you are! You're a lazy people, and that's why you say you want to go and sacrifice to your Lord. Go, get back to work. You'll get no straw, and you'll make the same number of bricks as you made yesterday!

And now the Hebrew foremen saw how things stood and that a bad time was coming. When they met Moses and Aaron, who were waiting outside Pharaoh's court, the foremen said, May the Lord look down and punish you for the trouble you have made for us. This is your fault! You made Pharaoh and his court hate us and have put a sword into their hand with which they will kill us!

⁂ ⁂ ⁂

MOSES WENT BACK TO THE LORD and said, Lord, why have You brought more trouble upon Your people? Why did you send me back? Since I spoke to Pharaoh in your name, he drives Your people harder, and You! You have not saved them!

The Lord said, Now you will see what

I shall do to Pharaoh! A mighty hand must force him to let My people go. Yes, by the force of My mighty hand he will drive them out of the land at last!

And God spoke to Moses and said, I am the Lord, the Almighty God. It was I who appeared to Abraham, to Isaac, and to Jacob. With them I made My covenant. To them I promised the land of Canaan, but it is to you that I make known My name: I AM THAT I AM. Yes, I hear the children of Israel groaning in their bondage under the Egyptian slave drivers. I shall snatch them out of the hand of the Egyptians and I shall judge Egypt with a great judgment. Egypt will know I am the Lord, and Israel will be My people, and I shall be their God.

Moses told Israel what the Lord had said, but they could not listen, because their hearts were too heavy. Their bondage was too hard for them to bear.

And the Lord said to Moses, Go to Pharaoh and tell him to let My people go.

But Moses said, If the children of Israel will not listen to me, why should Pharaoh listen to one whose speech is halting?

The Lord said, Look, you will command Pharaoh as if you were his God, and your brother Aaron will be your prophet. Say to Aaron everything I say to you and Aaron will say it to Pharaoh. And I shall harden Pharaoh's heart and he will not listen until I have performed great signs and wonders in the land of Egypt.

᙮   ᙮   ᙮

AND MOSES WAS EIGHTY YEARS OLD and Aaron was eighty-three, and the Lord said to them, When Pharaoh says, Let's see some of these wonders!—throw down your staff before his eyes, and the staff will turn into a snake!

Moses and Aaron went to Pharaoh and did what the Lord said. Aaron threw down his staff before the eyes of Pharaoh and all his court and it became a snake. But Pharaoh summoned his sorcerers, and each of the Egyptian sorcerers threw his staff down and all their staffs became snakes, but Aaron's staff swallowed up their staffs. But Pharaoh's heart hardened and he would not listen to them, as the Lord had said.

And the Lord said, Pharaoh's heart is hard and he will not let the people go. Tomorrow morning he will go to bathe. Stand on the bank of the Nile and when he comes out of the water go to him and say, The Lord, God of the Hebrews, has sent me to say, Let My people go into the

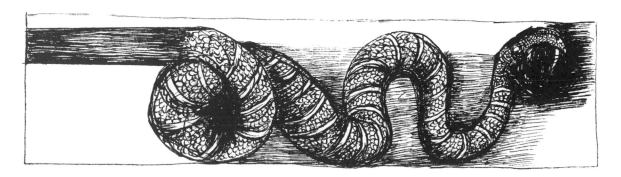

wilderness to worship Me. This is how you will know it is the Lord who has sent me: When I raise this staff that I carry in my hand and stretch out my hand and strike the water of the river, the water will turn to blood.

And Moses did as the Lord said and when he stretched out his hand and struck the water of the Nile before the eyes of Pharaoh and all his court, the water turned to blood, and the fish died in the Nile and in all the canals and in all the ponds in Egypt, and the Nile stank and the Egyptians could not drink the water, and all the water in every wooden bucket and every stone urn in all the land of Egypt turned to blood.

But the Egyptian sorcerers had their secret arts and did the same thing and they turned the water into blood, too, and Pharaoh's heart hardened. He went back to his palace and would not be moved, and everywhere in Egypt the people dug for water along the banks of the river Nile because they could not drink the blood.

⁂

WHEN SEVEN DAYS HAD PASSED, the Lord said to Moses, Go to Pharaoh and say, The Lord says, If you don't let My people go and worship Me, I will send a plague of frogs over the land. The Nile will swarm with frogs. They will climb out of the Nile and into your palace and into your bedroom and onto your bed, and into the houses of your courtiers and all your people, and into your ovens and your cooking pots. They will climb all over you and all your people and all your court.

The Lord told Moses and Moses told Aaron and Aaron stretched the staff in his hand over the rivers and canals and ponds and over all the waters of Egypt, and the frogs came out of the water and ran all over the land, but the Egyptian sorcerers did the same thing and made frogs come out of the water and run all over the land.

And Pharaoh sent for Moses and Aaron and said, Ask the Lord to take the frogs away and I will let your people go. You may go and make your sacrifice to the Lord!

Moses said, Tell me the time when you want me to ask the Lord to take the frogs away.

Pharaoh said, Tomorrow.

And Moses said, Tomorrow, when I ask the Lord, you and your court and all your people will be rid of every frog, except the frogs that are in the Nile, and you will know that there is no God like the Lord, our God.

Moses and Aaron left Pharaoh's palace, and Moses cried to the Lord to make good the promise he had made to Pharaoh, and all the frogs in all the houses, in the court-yards, and in the fields, died, and they piled up the dead frogs in great piles and the land stank.

Now Pharaoh had room to breathe, his heart hardened and he would not listen to Moses and Aaron, as the Lord had fore-told.

⁂

AND THE LORD SAID TO MOSES, Tell Aaron to hold out his staff and strike the dust of the earth and it will turn into lice in all the land of Egypt. And Aaron

stretched out his hand and struck the dust, and it turned into lice on man and beast throughout the land of Egypt. And the sorcerers did the same and tried all their secret spells, but they could not make lice. And the lice covered man and beast, and the sorcerers said to Pharaoh, This is the finger of God!

But Pharaoh's heart hardened and he would not listen, as the Lord had foretold.

≈ ≈ ≈

AND THE LORD SAID TO MOSES, Rise up early. Go and stand in front of Pharaoh as he comes down to the water and say, The Lord says, Let My people go and worship Me, or I will send vermin into your palace and into the houses of your courtiers and your people. All your houses and all the land will be filled with vermin. Only in the land of Goshen where My people live, there will be no vermin at all, because I distinguish between My people and your people, and it shall happen tomorrow.

And vermin filled Pharaoh's house and the houses of his court and of all the people in all the land of Egypt, and the land was ruined by the swarms of vermin.

Pharaoh sent for Moses and Aaron and said, All right. Sacrifice to your God, but do it here, in this land.

Moses said, It would not be good to do it here. The sacrifices we make to the Lord our God are abominations to the Egyptians. They would stone us. We must make a three-day journey into the wilderness. There we can sacrifice to the Lord our God, as He will command us.

Pharaoh said, I will let you go and sacrifice to the Lord your God in the wilderness, but don't go far, and pray for me!

Moses said, When I leave your presence, I will pray to the Lord, and tomorrow the vermin will be gone from Pharaoh's court and from his people. Only this time, don't deceive us! Don't keep us from going to make our sacrifices to the Lord.

And Moses left Pharaoh's presence and asked the Lord to take away the vermin, and the Lord took them away. Not a single one remained, and Pharaoh hardened his heart once again and he did not let the people go.

≈ ≈ ≈

THE LORD SAID TO MOSES, Go to Pharaoh and say, The Lord, God of the Hebrews, says, Let My people go and worship Me. If you prevent them, the hand of God will strike down the herds in your fields. He will bring down a plague upon your horses and upon your donkeys and your camels, and on your cattle and on your sheep and on your goats. But nothing shall die that belongs to the children of Israel in Goshen. And the Lord set the time, and said, That is what the Lord will do in this land tomorrow.

Next day all the animals of the Egyptians died, and Pharaoh sent his men to see, and it was true! Not one animal of the children of Israel had died! But Pharaoh's heart hardened and he did not let the people go.

≈ ≈ ≈

AND THE LORD SAID TO MOSES, Fill your hands with soot from the oven and throw it in the air in front of Pharaoh's eyes. The land of Egypt will be filled with fine dust that will make boils fester on man and beast in all the land of Egypt.

And he took soot from the oven and stood in front of Pharaoh and threw it toward heaven, and boils broke out on man and beast. The sorcerers could not appear before Moses because of the boils that covered them and every one of the Egyptians.

But the Lord hardened Pharaoh's heart and he would not listen, as the Lord had foretold.

The Lord said to Moses, Rise early in the morning. Go stand before Pharaoh and say, The Lord, the God of the Hebrews, says, Let My people go and worship Me, for this time I shall send down all My plagues upon you and upon your court and upon your people. I shall show you there is no one like Me in all the world. Don't you understand that I could stretch out My hand and wipe you and your people off the face of the earth? I have preserved you in order to show you the greatness of My might, and to make My name known upon the earth. This time tomorrow I shall send down a very great hailstorm. Egypt has seen nothing like it from the day of its foundation until this moment. Tell your people, Bring in your herds, for the hail will kill every man and every animal that is not brought in, and everything that is left out in the fields.

And those of Pharaoh's people who feared the word of the Lord ran and brought in their servants and their cattle, but those whose hearts did not fear God left their servants and their cattle out in the fields.

❧ ❧ ❧

AND THE LORD SAID TO MOSES, Stretch out your hand to heaven. Moses stretched out his staff to heaven and the Lord sent his thunder and hail upon Egypt, and the fire in the hail flashed from heaven down upon the earth. The hailstones were so heavy nothing like it had been seen in the land of Egypt since it had become a nation. The hail struck everything that was left out in all the fields of Egypt, man and beast, and knocked down every growing thing, and every tree was broken in the fields. Only in Goshen, where Israel lived, there was no hail.

And Pharaoh sent for Moses and Aaron and said, This time I have sinned. The Lord is right. I and my people are in the wrong. Ask the Lord to make an end of this thunder and hail, and I will let you go. You don't have to stay.

Moses said, When I go outside the city, I will raise my hands to the Lord, and the thunder will stop and there will be no more hail, and you will understand that the earth is the Lord's. But I know that you and your court still do not fear the Lord God.

When Pharaoh saw that the thunder and the rain had stopped he hardened his heart, he and all his court. He did not let Israel go, as the Lord had foretold.

❧ ❧ ❧

AND MOSES AND AARON WENT TO PHARAOH and said, The Lord, God of the Hebrews, says, How long will you refuse to bow before Me? Let My people go so they can worship Me. If you refuse to let My people go, I shall send a plague of locusts into your land. They will cover up the earth so that you will not see it. They will eat the little that the hail has left standing. They will eat the new growth off the trees out in your fields and they will fill your palace and the houses of your court and of all your people. Your fathers and the fathers of your fathers have seen nothing like it from the day they appeared upon the earth until this day.

And Moses turned and left Pharaoh's palace. And now the men of Pharaoh's court said, How much longer shall that man entrap us? Let the people go and worship their God. Do you want to wait till Egypt has gone under?

Moses and Aaron were called back, and Pharaoh said, Go, worship the Lord, your God. How many of you will be going?

Moses said, We will go with all our young and all the old, our sons and our daughters, and all our flocks and herds, so that we can make a feast to the Lord.

Pharaoh said, Yes indeed! And you think it's likely that I'm going to let you go and take your children! About as likely as your Lord going with you! You mean mischief! No! The men can go worship the Lord. Isn't that what you wanted? And they threw Moses out.

And the Lord said to Moses, Stretch your hand out over Egypt!

Moses stretched out his staff over Egypt and the Lord sent an east wind that blew all day and all night and in the morning the wind brought the locusts that settled everywhere on everything in Egypt. Never had there been, nor ever after will there be, so many locusts. They covered all the land and the ground was black with them. They devoured all the grass in the land and all the leaves on all the trees that the hail had left so that there was

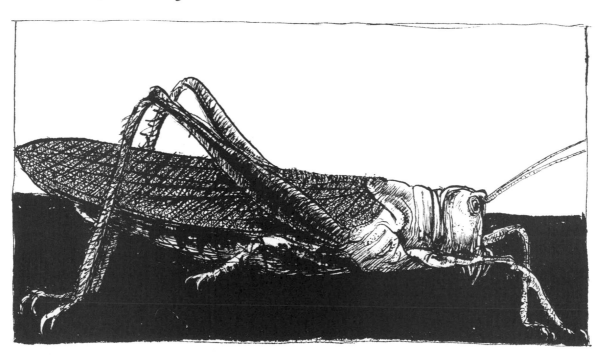

nothing green left on any tree or in any field in all the land of Egypt.

Pharaoh sent hurriedly for Moses and Aaron and said, I have sinned against the Lord your God and against you. Forgive my sin this one more time and ask the Lord your God to take this death away from me!

And Moses left Pharaoh and prayed, and the Lord turned the wind and it blew hard out of the west and picked up the locusts and drove them into the Red Sea until there was not a single locust left in all the land of Egypt.

But the Lord hardened Pharaoh's heart so that he would not let Israel go.

⁂

AND THE LORD SAID, Stretch out your hand to heaven and a darkness will descend on Egypt so thick you can touch it!

Moses stretched out his hand to heaven and the darkness that covered Egypt was so thick one could touch it. For three days no one could see his neighbor; no one could leave the place in which he happened to be.

Only in the houses of the Hebrews was it light.

Pharaoh sent for Moses and said, Go, worship the Lord, but leave your flocks and herds behind. Your children can go with you.

Moses said, And are you going to provide the animals for the burnt offering? Our cattle must go with us and not a hoof left behind. How can we know which animal to sacrifice until we get there?

But the Lord hardened Pharaoh's heart.

He would not let them go and said, Get out of my sight. The next time you see me, you shall die!

Moses answered, You're right. I shall never see your face again!

Now the Lord said, There is one more plague I shall bring upon Pharaoh and upon Egypt. Go speak in the ears of the children of Israel and tell them—both men and women—to ask their neighbor for a loan of gold and silver things. And the Lord made the Egyptians look kindly upon the children of Israel.

Besides, Moses was a great man in the eyes of the servants of Pharaoh and in the eyes of Israel. And Moses said to the children of Israel, The Lord says, At midnight I shall cross throughout the land of Egypt, and every firstborn in Egypt will die, from the firstborn son of Pharaoh, who sits on his throne, to the firstborn son of the slave girl who squats behind the mill, and every firstborn of every animal. And there will be such a wailing throughout all the land of Egypt as there has never been before nor will ever be again. But among the children of Israel not a dog will so much as snarl at man or beast.

⁂

AND THE LORD SPOKE TO MOSES AND AARON in Egypt and said, On the tenth day of this month let each man take a lamb—one lamb for every household. If there is a household too small for a whole lamb, let them share a lamb with their nearest neighbor and divide the lamb so there is enough for everyone to eat. On the fourteenth day of the month the congregation of Israel shall come together at twilight

festival to the Lord, you and your children and your children's children, and eat unleavened bread for seven days. He who eats leavened bread shall be cut off from the congregation of Israel. When you come to the land that the Lord will give you, keep this rite and when your children ask you, What is this rite for?—you shall say, It is the Passover sacrifice to the Lord, who passed over the houses of the children of Israel when he struck down the Egyptians and saved our houses. And the people bowed down and worshipped the Lord.

And at midnight the Lord struck down every firstborn in the land of Egypt, from the firstborn of Pharaoh, who sat upon his throne, to the firstborn of the prisoner in his dungeon, and every firstborn of the cattle. And Pharaoh rose in the night, and all his court, and all of the Egyptians. There was a great wailing in Egypt, for there was not a house in which someone had not died.

And Pharaoh summoned Moses and Aaron in the night and said, Get out of our land, you and the children of Israel. Go worship the Lord as you said. Take your herds and take your flocks as you said and go, and ask a blessing for me too.

Now the Egyptians hurried Israel out of Egypt, and said, Hurry up! If you don't get out of our land we are all of us going to die!

And the people had no time to prepare food for the journey and had to take the dough before it was leavened and they put it in their pots and wrapped it in their coats and loaded it onto their shoulders. And they took the silver and gold things

and slaughter the lambs. They shall take some of the blood and paint it on the doorposts and on the top of the door of the houses in which they will eat the lamb. You shall eat the lamb roasted, with unleavened bread and with bitter herbs, and with your coats on and tucked into your belts, with your shoes on your feet and your staff in your hands, hastily, for that will be the night of the Lord's Passover on which I shall cross through Egypt and strike down every firstborn—man and beast—and bring down My judgment upon the gods of Egypt, for I am the Lord. But the blood will be a sign that you are in the house. I will see the blood and pass over. And you shall remember this day and commemorate it with a

that Moses had told them to borrow from their neighbors, and that is how Israel stripped the Egyptians.

⁊   ⁊   ⁊

ISRAEL SET OUT FROM RAMESES to Succoth the morning after the Passover—about six hundred thousand men on foot—marching without fear in sight of the Egyptians burying their firstborn, whom the Lord had struck down in judgment upon the Egyptian gods. And there were many other sorts of people who went with them, as well as great droves of cattle. And the day the Lord brought the children of Israel out of their Egyptian bondage it was four hundred and thirty years to the day since they had come into the land of Egypt.

Now Pharaoh had let the children of Israel go. And God did not lead them through the land of the Philistines, which was the shorter way. God said in his heart, If war threatens they might turn around and go back to Egypt.

And Moses took Joseph's bones with him, because of the oath that Joseph had made the children of Israel swear to him when he said, God will surely come to you and you must carry my bones with you.

And they left Succoth and made camp in Etham on the edge of the wilderness.

And the Lord led the way in a pillar of cloud by day and by night in a pillar of fire to give them light, so that they could travel both by day and night, nor did He ever take the pillar of cloud nor the pillar of fire away from the people neither in the day nor in the night.

And the Lord spoke to Moses and said, Make camp in Pi-hahiroth by the Red Sea.

They came and told Pharaoh that Israel had fled, and Pharaoh and his court had a change of heart and said, What have we done? Why did we let Israel go? Who is going to serve us now?

And Pharaoh had them put horses to his chariot and took six hundred of his best chariots and all the rest of the chariots of Egypt, manned by his best warriors, and they pursued the children of Israel and overtook them where they camped by the Red Sea—Pharaoh and all his chariots and his horses and his army of warriors.

The children of Israel raised up their eyes—and there were the Egyptians coming after them! And Israel was afraid and cried aloud to the Lord. And to Moses they said, Were there no graves in Egypt that you brought us away to die in the wilderness? Didn't we ask you to leave us alone and let us serve the Egyptians? Better to serve in Egypt than die in the wilderness!

Moses said, Don't be afraid. Stand firm and watch the Lord's salvation which He will work for you today! You will never see the Egyptians again as you see them today. Stand still and the Lord will fight your fight.

The Lord said to Moses: Why do you come crying to Me? Tell Israel to march ahead. Raise your staff over the sea and divide it, and Israel will walk through the sea on dry ground. I shall harden the hearts of the Egyptians, and they will go in after you, and I will glorify Myself before Pharaoh and all his army of warriors and chariots and horsemen, and Egypt will know I am the Lord.

And the angel of God, who moved ahead of the Israelite army, went and stood in back of the camp; the pillar of cloud stood between the armies of Egypt and the armies of Israel, a cloud of darkness to one and a cloud of light to the other, and the two armies came no closer, one to the other.

And Moses stretched his hand over the sea and the Lord blew the sea back with a mighty wind out of the east that divided the water and drove it back, and the children of Israel walked through the middle of the sea on dry ground with a wall of water on their right and a wall of water on their left.

The Egyptians pursued them—all of Pharaoh's horses and his chariots and his horsemen went after them into the middle of the sea. At the morning watch the Lord looked out of the pillar of fire and cloud and threw them into confusion. He locked the wheels of their chariots so they could hardly move. The Egyptians said, Let us flee from the army of Israel! It is the Lord who fights for Israel against Egypt!

The Lord said to Moses, Stretch out your hand over the sea.

Moses stretched out his hand, and when day broke, the sea returned where it had always been. The Egyptians fled, but the Lord threw them back into the sea, and the water covered the chariots and all the warriors of the army of Pharaoh who had pursued Israel into the sea.

The children of Israel saw the Egyp-

tians dead along the shore, and they saw the mighty hand that the Lord had wielded against Egypt. And the people feared the Lord and put their trust in Him and in His servant Moses.

ᴁ ᴁ ᴁ

AND MOSES AND THE CHILDREN of Israel sang a song to the Lord: I will sing to the Lord! He raised Himself high and higher, hurling horse and rider into the sea. He is my victory song, yes, and my salvation, my God of safety. I will hold Him high and higher. A warrior God, the Lord is His name.

Pharaoh's chariots and all his might He hurled into the sea. The pick of his warriors sank in the Red Sea. The deep heaped upon them, water covered them. Like a stone they sank down.

Lord, Your right hand breaks the enemy. You shatter those who raise themselves against You. The heat of Your anger burns them like straw! The blast from Your nostrils piled the waters into walls in the heart of the sea.

The enemy boasted: I will pursue, I will overtake, I will divide the spoils; I will swallow them, I will draw my sword. My hand will destroy them!

A blast of Your breath, and the sea covered them. They sank like lead. Who among the gods is like You, glorious in your holiness, awesome in your splendor, performing wonders?

And the prophetess Miriam, the sister of Aaron and Moses, took a tambourine and the women followed with their tambourines, and danced in a ring, and

Miriam sang: Sing to the Lord, He raised himself high and higher, hurling horse and rider into the sea.

ᴁ ᴁ ᴁ

AND MOSES BROKE CAMP and led Israel from the Red Sea through the wilderness of Shur, a journey of three days, and they found no water, and came to Marah and could not drink the water because it was bitter. The people grumbled against Moses and said, What are we going to drink?

Moses cried to the Lord, and the Lord showed him a piece of wood, and Moses threw the wood into the water, and it made the water sweet.

And they went on and came to the wilderness of Sin and the people grumbled against Moses and Aaron and said, Would to God we had died in Egypt where we sat by our flesh pots with plenty of bread to eat! Have you brought us to this wilderness to starve this whole community to death?

And Moses and Aaron spoke to Israel and said, Know that the Lord, who brought you out of Egypt, hears you grumbling. You think you grumble against us, but who are we? It's not against us, it is against the Lord that you are grumbling!

And as they spoke these words the congregation of Israel looked toward the wilderness, and there it was! The glory of the Lord in a cloud!

And in the morning the dew lay round about the camp and when the dew was gone, Look! a layer of flakes like frost on the ground! The people saw it and did not know what it was and said to one another, What is it?

Moses said, It is the bread the Lord has given you to eat, and this is what the Lord has commanded you: Go out and gather what you need for the day and no more—one measure for every person in your tent.

The children of Israel gathered it up, and some gathered much and some gathered little, and when they measured it, the one who had gathered much had no more, and the one who had gathered little had no less—each had gathered as much as he needed to eat for the day.

Moses said, Keep nothing that is left over till the morning.

But there were those who did not listen to Moses and kept it until the morning, and it bred maggots and stank, and Moses was very angry. Each morning, each one gathered what he needed, and when the sun grew hot it melted away. On the sixth day Moses said, Tomorrow is the day of rest, a day sacred to the Lord. Gather two measures full. Bake it and cook it and lay it away until the morning.

And they laid away what was left, and in the morning it did not stink and had no maggots in it. Some who went out on the Sabbath found nothing. And the Lord said, How long will you refuse to follow My commandments and My laws?

They called it manna. It was white as coriander seed and tasted like cream made with honey, and that is what the children of Israel ate for forty years, until they came to inhabited land. Until they came to the borders of Canaan they ate manna.

≈ ≈ ≈

AND THE CONGREGATION of the children of Israel left the wilderness of Sin as God commanded them and came to Rephidim and pitched their tents. And the Amalekites came down upon Rephidim and fought with Israel.

Moses summoned Joshua and said, Choose some men and tomorrow you will go out and fight with the Amalekites. I shall stand on top of the hill with the staff of God in my hand.

And Joshua did as Moses said and went out to fight the Amalekites. Moses, Aaron, and Hur went up to the top of the hill, and as long as Moses held up his hand, Israel won, but when he let his hand sink, the Amalekites won. When Moses' hands grew heavy, they brought him a rock to sit on, and Aaron and Hur held up his hands—one on one side, one on the other.

And so his hands stayed up until the sun went down, and Joshua overpowered the Amalekite army with his sharp sword.

And the Lord said to Moses, Write this down in a book and remember it: I, the Lord, will punish the Amalekites and erase them from under the heavens!

And Moses built an altar to the Lord and called it the Lord is my banner from generation to generation.

※ ※ ※

MOSES' FATHER-IN-LAW JETHRO, the Midianite priest, heard what God had done for Moses and for Israel His people, and that the Lord had brought Israel out of Egypt. And Jethro took Zipporah, Moses' wife—for Moses had sent her back—and her two sons, and they came to meet Moses in the wilderness and sent him word: Jethro, your father-in-law, has come with your wife and her two sons.

Moses went out to meet his father-in-law and bowed low and kissed him, and when they had greeted each other they went into the tent. Moses told his father-in-law everything the Lord had done to Pharaoh and the Egyptians for Israel's sake, and about the hardships they had met along the way, and how the Lord had saved them.

Jethro rejoiced and said, Praise to the Lord! Now I know He is greater than all the gods. And Jethro offered a burnt offering for God, and Aaron and all the elders of Israel came and ate with Moses' father-in-law.

The next morning Moses took his judge's seat, and the people stood around Moses from morning till evening.

Jethro watched and said, What are you doing, acting all by yourself, with people around you from morning till evening?

Moses said, When they quarrel they come to me. I judge between one man and another and make God's laws known to them.

Moses' father-in-law said, What you are doing isn't right. You'll wear yourself out and you will wear out this people. It's too much for you. You can't do it alone. Listen to the advice I'm going to give you, and may God be with you. You're the one who must teach Israel the laws of God and how to follow them and what they must do. But look among your people for able men who fear God and hate dishonest gain. Appoint them as chiefs over groups of a thousand, a hundred, fifty, and ten people. The hard cases they will bring to you. Let them judge in small matters. It will make it easier for you, and they'll carry part of your burden. If you do this, and it is what God wants, you will last out the task God has given you, and the people will get where they are going in peace.

Moses listened to his father-in-law and did everything he said, and Jethro went home to his own country.

※ ※ ※

AND THE CHILDREN OF ISRAEL left Rephidim and came to the wilderness of Sinai and camped at the foot of the mountain.

And Moses went up to God, and the Lord called to him out of the mountain and said, This is what you shall say to the house of Israel: Your eyes have seen what I have done to the Egyptians in Egypt for your sake, how I have carried you on eagles' wings to bring you to Me. Listen to My voice, keep My covenant, and you shall be My particular treasure among the nations, for all the earth is Mine. You shall be a kingdom of priests to Me and a holy nation.

And Moses came down and called the elders of the people and laid before them these words, which the Lord had commanded him to say. And the people said with one voice, We will do everything the Lord has said! All that the Lord has said, we will do.

Moses carried the people's answer to the Lord. And the Lord said, I shall come to you in the thickness of a cloud and the people will hear Me speak to you and will believe you forever. Go down. Tell them to purify themselves today. Tomorrow let them wash their clothing and be ready for the third day, for on the third day the Lord shall come down onto Mount Sinai before the eyes of all the people. But make sure that the people keep their distance. Take care that no one comes up the mountain or so much as touches its lowest part. Whoever touches the mountain must assuredly be put to death; let no hand touch him. He shall be stoned to death with stones or pierced with the spear, man or beast, he shall not live.

And it happened on the third day in the morning, that there was thunder and lightning, and a thick cloud covered the mountain, and a trumpet blasted exceedingly loud. The people in the camp trembled. Moses brought the children of Israel out of the camp to meet with God, and they stood at the foot of the mountain.

And Mount Sinai was all smoke, for the Lord had descended in fire upon it, and the smoke rose like the smoke from a furnace, and the mountain rocked, the blast of the trumpet grew loud and louder. And Moses spoke and God answered him in thunder.

And the people moved back from the thunder and lightning and the blasting trumpet and the smoking mountain. They said to Moses, You speak to us. We will do what you say, only don't let God speak to us, or we shall die!

Moses said, Don't be afraid. It is only God coming to test you, so that you will fear Him and not sin.

And the people stood at a distance, and the Lord called Moses to come up and Moses went into the darkness and there was God, and a pavement at His feet as if it had been made of sapphire, and a brightness like the heart of heaven.

≈　≈　≈

GOD SAID, These are the ten commandments which you shall teach the children of Israel:

I am the Lord your God who brought you out of the land of Egypt, and out of slavery.

Have no other gods besides Me. Make yourself no idols nor any image of anything that is in the heavens above or on the earth below, or in the water under the earth. Do not bow down to them or serve them, for I, the Lord your God, am a jealous God and will punish the children for the sins of the fathers down to the third and fourth generation of those who hate Me, but show mercy to the thousandth generation of those who love Me and keep My commandments.

Do not use the name of the Lord your God in vain. The Lord will not forgive those who use His name in vain.

Remember the Sabbath day, and keep it holy. You shall labor and do all your work in six days, but the seventh day is the Sabbath of the Lord your God. On that day you shall not work, neither you, nor your son, nor your daughter, nor your manservant nor your maidservant, nor your cattle, nor the stranger in your city, for in six days the Lord made the heavens and the earth and the sea, and all that is in them, and on the seventh day He rested; therefore the Lord blessed the Sabbath day and made it holy.

Honor your father and your mother, so you may live long on the land which the Lord your God gives to you.

Do not kill.

Do not commit adultery.

Do not steal.

Do not bear false witness against your neighbor.

Do not covet your neighbor's house, nor his wife, nor his manservant nor his maidservant, nor his ox nor his ass, nor anything that belongs to your neighbor.

And again the Lord said to Moses, Come up the mountain to Me. Be there. I will give you the tablets of stone on which I have written the law which you shall teach the children of Israel.

And Moses rose and his servant Joshua went with him to the mountain of God, and Moses said to the elders, Wait here until we come back. Look, you have Aaron and Hur here with you. If you have a question of law you can turn to them.

Moses went up and a cloud covered the mountain, and the presence of the Lord was on Mount Sinai; the cloud covered the mountain for six days, and on the seventh day He called Moses out of the cloud. And to the children of Israel the Presence of the Lord appeared like a devouring fire on the top of the mountain. And Moses went into the middle of the cloud and was on the mountain forty days and forty nights.

⁌ ⁌ ⁌

WHEN THE PEOPLE SAW that Moses was not coming down from the mountain, they gathered together and they came to Aaron and said, Come on! Make us a god whom we can follow. As for that Moses who brought us out of Egypt—who knows what's become of him!

Aaron said, Pull the golden rings from the ears of your wives and your sons and your daughters and bring them to me.

The people pulled the rings out of their ears and brought them to Aaron, and Aaron took them and molded a calf. The people said, This, O Israel, is your god, who brought you out of the land of Egypt!

Aaron saw what they were doing and built an altar for the calf and proclaimed, Tomorrow there shall be a festival to the Lord.

The people rose early and offered burnt offerings and brought peace offerings to the golden calf, and they sat down to eat and drink and stood up to dance and sing.

And the Lord said to Moses, Go, get yourself back down there! Your people, whom you brought out of Egypt, have corrupted themselves! How quickly they have turned away from My commandments. They have made themselves a golden calf and bow down and offer it burnt offerings, and say, This, O Israel, is your god, who brought you out of the land of Egypt! And the Lord said, I know them! They are a stiff-necked people! Leave Me alone, so I can let My anger rage and destroy them!

And Moses pleaded with the Lord and said, O Lord! Why does Your anger rage against Your own people, whom You brought out of Egypt with the might of Your great hand? Do You want the Egyptians to say, It was to do them mischief that He brought them out, so He could slay them in the mountain and wipe them off the face of the earth! Relent Your rage against them. Remember Your servants Abraham, Isaac, and Jacob, to whom You swore by Your Self, saying, I shall make your descendants numerous as the stars in the sky and give the land I have promised them to be their inheritance forever.

And the Lord relented and did not punish the children of Israel as he had threatened.

And Moses turned and went down the mountain, and in his hand were the two tablets of the law, with writing on both sides, front and back, and it was God's own work—the writing was God's writing engraved on the tablets.

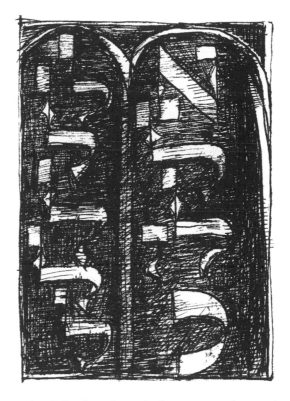

And Joshua heard the noise of people shouting and said, There are sounds of war in the camp!

But Moses said, Those are not the sounds of people shouting for victory, nor the shout of defeat. I hear people singing!

They came closer and saw the calf and the people dancing around it, and Moses' anger flared. He threw down the tablets at the foot of the mountain and broke them in pieces. And Moses took the calf that they had made and burned it in the fire, and ground it to powder, and strewed it on the water, and made the children of Israel drink it.

To Aaron he said, What did these people do, that you have brought so great a sin upon them?

Aaron said, Don't be angry, my lord! You yourself know this people, how prone they are to evil! They said, Come on, make us a god whom we can follow. As for that Moses, who brought us out of Egypt—who knows what's become of him!

So I said, Whoever has gold, take it off. And they brought it to me and I threw it in the fire, and out came this calf!

Moses saw that Aaron had let the people run wild. He went and stood by the gates of the camp and said, All those on the side of the Lord, come here.

And all the sons of Levi gathered around Moses and Moses said, This is the word of the Lord, the God of Israel: Let every one of you gird on his sword and go through the camp from one end to the other and slay his brother, his neighbor, his kin.

And they did as Moses said. Some three thousand of the people died that day. And Moses said to them, Bow down to the Lord, for each one of you has raised your hand against your son, and your brother. May the Lord give you His blessing.

Next day Moses spoke to the people and said: You have committed a great sin. I will go up to the Lord and ask His forgiveness.

Moses went back to the Lord and said, Great is the sin the people have committed against You! They have made themselves a god out of gold! Forgive them their sin, or blot me out, too, from Your book which You have written!

The Lord said, I blot out only him who has sinned against Me. Now go down. Lead the people as I have commanded you. I will send an angel to go ahead of you and lead you to the land flowing with milk and honey that I have promised to give your descendants. I will drive out the Canaanites, the Amorites, the Hittites, the Perizzites, the Hivites, and the Jebusites. But I shall not go with you for you are a stiff-necked people. If I went with you I would destroy you on the way. If I came among you for so much as the wink of an eye, I would wipe you off the face of the earth! Say to Israel, Take off your finery until I decide what to do with you! The day I come among you will be the day I come to punish Israel's sin.

⁂ ⁂ ⁂

AND MOSES TOOK UP HIS TENT and pitched it at a distance from the camp and called it the Tent of the Congregation. Whoever wanted to ask the Lord's counsel went out to the tent. Whenever Moses left the camp, the people came and stood at the doors of their tents and watched him until he entered the tent and the pillar of cloud came down and stood at the door, and the Lord spoke with Moses, face to face, like a man speaking with his friend.

Moses said to the Lord, Look, Lord, You have told me to lead this people, but You don't say whom You will send to go with me.

The Lord said, It is My Presence that will go before you. It will lighten your burden.

Moses said, Never let us leave this place unless Your Presence goes before us. What distinguishes us from every other people on the face of the earth is only Your Presence in our midst!

The Lord said, I will do what you ask

Me to do, because you have found favor in My eyes, and I call you by your name.

Moses said, Lord, let me look upon the glory of Your Presence!

And He answered: I will let My goodness pass before your eyes and I will proclaim to you the name of the Lord. I show My favor to whom I show My favor, and My mercy to whom I show My mercy. And He said, You may not see My face. No man may see Me and live. And He said, Look! Here is a place, by Me. Stand on this rock and when My glory passes by you, I will put you in a cleft of the rock and cover you with My hand till I have passed. And I will take away My hand, and you shall see My back, but My face may not be seen.

≈ ≈ ≈

AND THE LORD SAID, Carve two stone tablets like the first, and I will write down the words that were on the first tablets, which you broke in pieces. Be ready tomorrow morning and come to Mount Sinai and stand before Me. Let no one come up with you.

Moses carved two stone tablets like the first and rose early and went up to Mount Sinai, as the Lord had commanded him, and had the two stone tablets in his hand.

And the Lord descended in a cloud and was with Moses, and passing before the face of Moses, He pronounced the name of the Lord, and proclaimed, The Lord, the Lord God, merciful and gracious, slow to anger, full of love and faithful for a thousand generations, forgiving iniquity and transgression, who will not let the guilty go free but shall bring the sins of

the fathers upon the children and the children's children to the third and fourth generations.

And the Lord said, Write down these words, for according to these words I make My covenant with you and with Israel.

And Moses was with the Lord forty days and forty nights and ate no bread and drank no water. He wrote down on the tablets the words of the Lord's covenant.

When Moses came down from Mount Sinai he had the tablets in his hands and did not know that the skin of his face shone from speaking with God.

Aaron and the children of Israel saw Moses and the skin of his face shone, and they were afraid to come near him. Moses called to them and to Aaron and to the

elders of Israel, and they went to him. He spoke with them and gave them the commandments that the Lord had given him on Mount Sinai.

When Moses had finished speaking, he covered his face with a veil. And whenever Moses went in to speak with the Lord he took the veil from his face, but when he came out to tell the children of Israel what the Lord had commanded him, the skin of his face shone and he covered his face, until he went back to speak with the Lord.

And the cloud covered the tent and the Presence of the Lord filled the tabernacle.

When the cloud lifted from the tent, the children of Israel went on with their journey, but if the cloud did not lift, they waited until it lifted.

≈ ≈ ≈

AND THE LORD SPOKE TO MOSES and said, Instruct Aaron how he shall bless the children of Israel. He shall say:

The Lord bless you and keep you.

The Lord make His face to shine upon you and be gracious to you.

The Lord turn His face upon you and give you peace.

And the Lord said, When you lay My name upon the children of Israel, I shall bless them.

≈ ≈ ≈

AND THE CLOUD LIFTED from the Tent of the Congregation, and Israel set out from the wilderness of Sinai and went from place to place until the cloud came to rest in the wilderness of Paran. And the Lord

heard how the people grumbled and His anger burned against them and the Lord's fire fed on the outskirts of the camp. The people cried to Moses, and Moses prayed to the Lord, and the fire died down.

But the rabble among the people began to crave other kinds of food. Israel wept and said, Who will give us meat? Remember the fish we used to eat in Egypt—and it didn't cost a thing! And the cucumbers and melons, the leeks, the onions, the garlic! The soul dries up when all you ever see is this manna!

The manna tasted like coriander and was the color of resin. The people ran around and gathered it up, pounded and ground it in handmills, or crushed it in a mortar, and boiled it in pots, or made it into cakes. It tasted of cream of oil. And every night when the dew fell, the manna came down on the camp.

Moses heard the people weeping, every man standing at the door of his tent, and he was troubled and said, Lord, have I lost my Lord's favor that You lay the burden of all this people upon me? Did I conceive this people! Did I give them birth! Why do I have to carry them in my arms, like a nurse carrying a baby, all the way to the promised land? Where shall I get meat for all this people? They come crying to me, and say, Give us meat! It's too much for me! I can't carry this whole people alone! Kill me here and now, I beg you, so I don't have to see my own wretchedness.

The Lord said, Choose seventy of the elders of Israel and bring them to the Tent of the Congregation. I shall take a measure of the spirit that is upon you and lay it upon them. They will help you bear the burden of this people so that you will not have to carry it alone.

And the Lord said, Speak to the people and say, You shall have meat to eat. The Lord has heard you weeping and He will give you meat to eat, not for one day, or two days, or five, or ten or twenty days, but every day for a month until it comes out of your nostrils and you can't bear the sight of it, because you scorn the Lord, who is among you, and you cry and you say, Why did we ever leave Egypt?

Moses said, Lord, I have six hundred thousand men with me, and You say, I will give them meat to eat for a whole month! Who can slaughter enough flocks and herds to feed them? If one caught every fish in the sea would it be enough?

The Lord said, Has the Lord's arm grown so short? Now you shall see if My word shall come true or not.

Moses summoned seventy of the elders of Israel and made them stand around the tent. And the Lord took a measure of the spirit of Moses and laid it upon the seventy elders, and the Spirit came to rest on them and they prophesied though afterward they never did so again.

There were two of the elders who did not come out to the Tent of the Congregation but stayed inside the camp, yet the Spirit came to rest on them, too, and they prophesied in the camp.

A boy came running and told Moses, Eldad and Medad are prophesying in the camp!

Joshua, who had been Moses' attendant since his youth, cried, My lord, Moses, make them stop!

But Moses said, Are you jealous for me, Joshua? I wish all the Lord's people were prophets, that the Lord might lay His Spirit upon them!

And the wind from the Lord drove in quail from the sea and let them fall around the camp to a height of three feet as far as a day's walk in each direction. All that day and night and all the next day the people went about and gathered quail. No one gathered less than ten measures. They spread the quail all around the camp to dry. But the meat was still between their teeth when the Lord's anger rekindled against the people and He struck them with a plague, and the place is called Kibroth-Hattaavah, meaning graves of craving.

From Kibroth-Hattaavah the children of Israel went on to Hazeroth and pitched their tents.

※   ※   ※

AND MIRIAM AND AARON began to talk against Moses, because he had taken an Ethiopian wife. They said, Does the Lord speak only through Moses? Doesn't He speak through us, as well? And the Lord heard what they said.

Now Moses was a very humble man, the most humble man on the face of the earth.

Suddenly the Lord said to Moses and Aaron and Miriam, Come out, all three of you, to the Tent of the Congregation. The three went out, and the Lord descended in a pillar of cloud and stood at the door of the tent and called, Aaron! Miriam!

The two stood before Him, and He

said; Hear My words. When there is a prophet of the Lord among you I make Myself known to him in visions and speak to him in dreams, but My servant Moses is a familiar within My household. With him I speak not in riddles but mouth to mouth. He looks upon the likeness of the Lord. And are you not afraid to speak against My servant Moses? The Lord was very angry with them and He went away, and when the cloud lifted from the tent, Miriam stood there a leper, as if she had been encrusted with snow. Aaron turned, and look! She was a leper! Aaron said to Moses, Don't, my lord, hold our foolish sin against us! Don't let Miriam live like one who is dead, like a stillborn infant that comes out of its mother's womb with its flesh eaten half away!

And Moses cried to the Lord and said, O God, heal her, I beg You!

The Lord said, If her father had spit in her face, would she not suffer seven days of shame, at the least? Let her be shut out from the camp for seven days, then you may take her back.

And Miriam was shut out from the camp for seven days, and the people did not move on until she was taken back.

After this the children of Israel left Hazeroth and pitched their tents in the wilderness of Paran.

≈ ≈ ≈

AND THE LORD SPOKE TO MOSES and said, Send twelve men into Canaan to spy out the land.

And Moses sent out twelve men, the chiefs of the twelve tribes of Israel. One of them was called Caleb and one was Joshua. And Moses said to them, Go south, up into the hill country. See what kind of land it is—if the people are strong or weak, few or many, if the land is good or poor, and if the towns in which they live are fortified, if the soil is rich or thin, wooded or not. You must be brave. And bring back some of the fruit that grows there.

And they went up from the wilderness and spied out the land. They cut down a branch of a vine that bore a single cluster

of grapes, and two of them had to carry it between them on a pole. They found pomegranates and figs, and they spied for forty days and returned to the wilderness of Paran and reported what they had seen to Moses and Aaron and to the whole congregation. They said, We have been in the land to which you sent us, and it is true! It flows with milk and honey, and this is the fruit that grows there, but the people are very powerful! Their cities are fortified and very large. And we saw giants! The Amalekites live in the south; the Hittites, the Jebusites, and the Amorites in the hills; and the Canaanites have settled on the coast and along the Jordan.

Caleb wanted to calm the people for Moses and said, Let us go up—let's go up at once, and take the land! We can easily overcome them!

But the other spies said, How are we going to fight them? They are too strong for us! And they spread rumors among the children of Israel and said, It is a land that will devour anyone who tries to settle in it! The people we saw are immense. They are the sons of a race of giants. They made us feel like grasshoppers, and that's what we must have looked like to them!

Now the people cried aloud. All night they wept and railed against Moses and said, If God had only let us die in Egypt! If only we might die in the wilderness! Will the Lord lead us into this land to die by the sword? They'll carry off our wives and our little children! Better to return to Egypt! And they said to one another, Let's choose ourselves a leader and go back to Egypt.

Now Moses and Aaron threw themselves down on the ground before all the people, and Joshua and Caleb tore their clothes and said, It is a very good land! If the Lord is pleased with us He will lead us into that land, and give it to us, a land flowing with milk and honey! Only don't set yourselves against the Lord! You have nothing to fear from those people! We're going to eat them for our supper. What defense do they have if the Lord is on our side? There is nothing to be afraid of!

The people wept and would have stoned them, but over the Tent of the Congregation there appeared the Glory of His Presence, and the Lord spoke to Moses, and said, How long will this people scorn Me and rail against Me, after all the wonders which I have done among them? I shall strike them with a plague. I disinherit them, and out of you I will make a nation more mighty and more numerous than they!

But Moses said, The Egyptians have heard how You have brought this people out from among them. When they hear it rumored that You mean to kill this people to the last man, they'll say, It was beyond His power to bring them into the land which He promised them under His oath, and that's why He slaughtered them in the wilderness. Therefore, Lord, let Your power show in its greatness according to Your word. You have said, The Lord is slow to anger and full of mercy, forgiving iniquity and transgression, yet He does not let the guilty go free but shall bring the sins of the fathers upon the children to the third and fourth generation. Now let the greatness of your mercy forgive this people its iniquity.

And the Lord said, I forgive them because you ask Me! But as surely as I live, and as My Presence fills the earth, not one of those whose eyes have seen the Glory of My Presence and the wonders that I have done for them in Egypt, and in the wilderness, and who have tried Me ten times over and have disobeyed Me and railed against Me—not a single one shall see the land I promised to their fathers. Only Caleb and Joshua, whose spirit has been faithful to Me, will I bring into the promised land. As for these grumblers and railers, this is what you shall say to them: Your carcasses shall rot in the wilderness! Every one of you who is twenty years or more and has railed against the Lord—know this: not one of you shall enter the land! You said, The enemy will carry off our little children! These same children shall enter the land that you have held so cheap but your carcasses shall rot. Forty years—one year for each of the forty days the spies spied out the promised land—shall you wander in the wilderness until it grinds you down to nothing! I am the Lord. I have spoken.

As for those whom Moses had sent to spy out the land and brought back evil rumors and misled the people and set them grumbling—they died of the plague. Only Joshua and Caleb were left alive.

Moses told the children of Israel what the Lord had said and they wept, and they rose early next morning and went up into the hills and said, Here we are, ready to go into the promised land! We were in the wrong.

But Moses said, Again you disobey the words of the Lord and no good can come of this. Do not go now, because now the Lord is not with you, and your enemy will rout you.

But they would not listen and went up, and the Amalekites and the Canaanites came down and routed and dispersed them.

≈ ≈ ≈

AND IT HAPPENED on a Sabbath that they found a man gathering wood in the wilderness, and they brought him before Moses and Aaron and the whole congregation and kept him imprisoned because there was no decree that said what was to be done with him. And the Lord spoke to Moses and said, The man must die. The whole congregation shall take him outside the camp and stone him to death.

And the whole congregation took him outside the camp and stoned him to death as the Lord had commanded Moses.

≈ ≈ ≈

AND KORAH of the house of Levi, together with two hundred and fifty Israelites, men of standing in the congregation, gathered against Moses and Aaron and said to them, you overreach yourselves. The congregation is holy. Why do you raise yourselves above all the rest of us? When Moses heard this, he fell with his face to the ground and said, Tomorrow the Lord will make known who is His and who may approach Him. You go too far, you Levites! Isn't it enough that the God of Israel has set you apart within the congregation of Israel, and chosen you to serve Him in His tabernacle! And do you want to be His priests as well? You think you grumble against Aaron, but it is the Lord against whom you have gathered together, you and all your followers! And Moses said, Take your censers. Fill them with fire and incense. Tomorrow you, your followers, and Aaron shall appear before the Lord. We shall see whom the Lord will choose.

And each man brought his censer and put in fire and incense, and took his place at the door of the Tent of the Congregation, and the Presence of the Lord appeared before the whole congregation, and there came a fire from the Lord and consumed the two hundred and fifty followers of Korah where they stood with their censers.

⁂ ⁂ ⁂

AND NOW DATHAN AND ABIRAM of the house of Reuben rose up against Moses. And Moses summoned Dathan and Abiram, but they said, We're not coming! Isn't it enough that you have taken us away from Egypt, a land flowing with milk and honey, to kill us out here in the wilderness? Now you want to make yourself a prince and lord it over us! Where's this promised land? Where are these fields and vineyards to pass on to our children! Now what do you want with us? Are you going to gouge our eyes out? We are not coming!

Moses' anger burned and he said, Have I ever taken so much as a single ass of theirs? What wrong have I ever done any one of them!

And the Lord spoke to Moses and Aaron and said, Stand away from the congregation. I will destroy it here and now.

But Moses fell down with his face to the ground and said, O God of the spirit of all flesh! Will you be angry with a whole congregation because of the sin of these men!

The Lord said, Tell the people to stand away from the tents of Dathan and Abiram.

And Moses spoke to the children of Israel and said: Stand away from the tents of these wicked men! Touch nothing that belongs to any one of them, or you will be destroyed for their sins!

The people moved away. Only Dathan and Abiram came out with their wives, their children, and their little ones and stood in the doors of their tents.

Moses said, Now you will see that the Lord has sent me to do these things and that I have not done them of my own choosing. If these men die, like other men, and meet a natural end, like all mankind, then it was not the Lord who has sent me. But if the Lord makes something new happen, if the earth opens its wide mouth and swallows them and everything that belongs to them, and they go down alive into the grave, then you will know that they are men who have scorned the Lord.

And as he finished speaking, it happened that the earth tore apart under them, where they stood, and opened up its wide mouth and swallowed them with all their households and their people and everything that belonged to them, and they went down into the grave alive and the earth closed over them. They dis-

appeared out of the middle of the congregation. The children of Israel who stood around them fled from their screaming and thought, What if the earth swallows us as well!

Next day the whole congregation of Israel grumbled against Moses and Aaron, and said, You have killed the people of the Lord! And they looked and saw the cloud that covered the Tent of the Congregation and the Presence of the Lord appeared.

Moses and Aaron fell with their faces to the ground and Moses said to Aaron, Go quickly! Take your censer, fill it with fire from the altar, and make atonement for the sins of this congregation, for the Lord's anger has begun its work. The plague has come into the camp.

Aaron ran among the congregation and offered incense to the Lord and made atonement and stood between the dead and the living, and the plague stopped. Fourteen thousand and seven hundred people had died, besides those who died with Korah and with Dathan and Abiram.

✵ ✵ ✵

AND THE CHILDREN OF ISRAEL came to the wilderness of Zin and pitched their tents at Kadesh. And there Miriam died and was buried.

And there was no water for the people and they quarreled with Moses and with Aaron and said, If only we had died with our brothers! And, Why did you bring us to die in this wilderness together with all our cattle! And, Why did you take us out of Egypt and bring us into this terrible place, a place where there's no corn, and no figs, no grapevines, no pomegranates, not even water for us to drink!

Moses and Aaron turned away from them and went to the door of the Tent of the Congregation and fell down with their faces to the ground, and the Presence of the Lord appeared before them. The Lord said to Moses, Take your staff and gather the people, and speak to the rock for all the people to see, and the rock will give you water. You will make water come out of the rock and give the people and their cattle to drink.

But Moses took the Lord's staff, and gathered the people and said, Listen, you rebellious people! Shall I make water flow out of this rock? And he lifted his hand and with his staff he struck the rock twice, and water flowed out of the rock, and the community and all their herds drank.

But the Lord spoke to Moses and Aaron and said, Because you did not

believe in Me, and did not sanctify Me in the eyes of Israel, you shall not lead this people into the land that I shall give them!

≈ ≈ ≈

AND MOSES SENT MESSENGERS to the king of Edom saying, A greeting from your brother Israel! You know the hardships we have suffered, how our forefathers went down into Egypt, how long we were in Egypt, how harshly the Egyptians treated us, and how we cried out to the Lord. He heard our voice and sent an angel to lead us out of Egypt. We are here, in Kadesh, close to your border. We ask your leave to pass through your country. We will not go through your fields or vineyards, nor will we drink the water from your wells. We will keep on the king's highway nor stray right or left until we have passed through your territory.

But Edom answered, You shall not pass through, or I will come out to meet you with the sword.

The children of Israel answered, We will stay on the beaten track; if we or our herds drink your water, we will pay for it. Only let us pass on foot—that's all!

Edom said, You are not passing here! And he marched against Israel with many of his people, heavily armed. Israel turned and went the other way and left Kadesh and came to Mount Hor.

And there the Lord spoke with Moses and Aaron and said, Aaron must die and be gathered to his people. He will not enter the promised land because you disobeyed the word of My mouth by the waters of Meribah. Go up to Mount Hor. Take off Aaron's garments and put them on his son Eleazar, for Aaron will be gathered to his fathers and die on Mount Hor.

When Moses and Eleazar came down from the mountain the congregation of Israel knew that Aaron was dead and Israel wept for thirty days.

≈ ≈ ≈

WHEN KING ARAD, the Canaanite, heard that Israel was on its way coming toward him he attacked them and took prisoners, and Israel swore an oath to the Lord, and said, If You will deliver this people into our hands, we will destroy their cities utterly!

And the Lord heard the voice of Israel and delivered the Canaanites into their hands, and they destroyed them and all their cities utterly. And the place is called Hormah, meaning utter destruction.

From Mount Hor they moved on to the Red Sea, and went around Edom, and the people lost heart and grumbled against God and against Moses, and said, Why have you brought us out of Egypt to die in the wilderness? There is no bread and no water, and this miserable manna we eat is making us sick!

And the Lord sent poisonous snakes to bite the people, and many died, and they came to Moses and said, We were wrong to speak against the Lord and against you. Pray the Lord to take these snakes away!

And Moses prayed for the people. And the Lord said, Make a snake and put it on a pole. If anyone is bitten let him look at the snake and he will live. And Moses made a snake out of copper and put it on a pole and if anyone was bitten he looked at the copper snake and lived.

≈ ≈ ≈

AND THE CHILDREN OF ISRAEL moved on and pitched their tents in Oboth, and left Oboth and moved on to Iye-abarim in the wilderness to the east of Moab. They moved on and came into the valley in the country of Moab and to the top of Mount Pisgah that looks over the wasteland. And Israel sent messengers to Sihon, king of the Amorites, saying, Let me pass through your country.

But Sihon would not let Israel pass through, but gathered his people and came out against Israel in the wilderness. And Israel put them to the sword and took their land from the Arnon to the Jabbok and occupied their cities.

And Og, king of Bashan, came out against Israel with all his people. The Lord said, You have nothing to fear! I put him into your hand with all his people and all his land. Do to him as you did to Sihon, king of the Amorites! And they vanquished King Og and his sons and all his people, and left not one alive and took possession of his land.

And the children of Israel moved on and pitched their tents in the plains of Moab, on the other side of the Jordan across from Jericho.

≈ ≈ ≈

AND BALAK, king of the Moabites, saw what Israel had done to the Amorites and was terrified because there were so many

of them. Balak had a horror of the children of Israel, and said to the elders of Midian, They will chew up everything around us like an ox chewing the grass in the field.

King Balak sent a message to Balaam, who lived at Pethor, by the river Euphrates, saying, There's a people that has come up from Egypt. There are so many they cover the face of the earth, and they have pitched their tents across from here. They are too strong for me. Come at once and curse this people for me so that I can beat them and drive them from the land. I know those whom you bless are blessed, and whom you curse are accursed.

The elders of Moab and the elders of Midian took with them money to pay for divination, and came to Balaam, and gave him Balak's message.

Balaam said, Stay here tonight; I will give you the answer that the Lord will give me. And so the princes of Moab stayed that night with Balaam.

God came to Balaam and said, Who are these men with you?

Balaam said, Balak, the king of Moab, has sent me a message saying, There's a people that has come up from Egypt; there are so many they cover the face of the earth. Come at once and curse this people for me so that I can beat them and drive them from the land.

God said, You shall not go with them! You shall not curse them; they are a blessed people.

In the morning Balaam rose and he said, Go back to your country. The Lord will not let me go with you.

The princes of Moab rose and returned to Balak and said, Balaam would not come with us.

This time Balak sent more and greater princes than the first. They came to Balaam and said, Balak says, Do not refuse me, please, but come! I will reward you honorably. I will do whatever you say. Only come and curse this people for me!

Balaam said, If Balak gives me a house full of silver and gold I can do nothing, whether large or small, that goes against the Lord's commandment. But you can stay here tonight until I know what the Lord my God will say this time.

God came to Balaam in the night and said, Because these men have come to ask you to go with them, go, but say only what I tell you to say.

Balaam rose in the morning, saddled his ass, and went with the princes of Moab. But it angered God that he went with them and an angel of the Lord came and stood in the road to bar his way. Balaam was riding his ass and had two servants with him, and the ass saw the angel of the Lord standing in the way, a sword drawn in his hand, and the ass stepped off the road into the field. Balaam beat her to get her back on the road. But the angel of the Lord went ahead and stood in the narrow path between the vineyards with a fence on this side and a fence on that side. The ass saw the angel of the Lord and squeezed herself against the fence and squeezed

Balaam's foot, and Balaam beat her again. And again the angel of the Lord went ahead and stood in a place so narrow there was no room to turn right or left. The ass saw the angel of the Lord and she lay down underneath Balaam. Balaam was so angry he beat the ass with his stick.

And the Lord opened the ass's mouth, and she said, What did I do that you have beaten me these three times?

Balaam said, You're playing tricks on me! If I had my sword in my hand, I'd kill you here and now!

The ass said, Aren't I your own ass? How long have you been riding me? Am I in the habit of doing this kind of thing?

He said, No.

Now the Lord opened Balaam's eyes, and he saw the angel of the Lord standing in the way with the sword drawn in His hand, and Balaam bowed down with his face to the ground.

The angel of the Lord said, Why did you beat your ass these three times? Look! I have come to bar your way because it goes against Me. Your ass saw Me and stepped out of My way these three times. If she had not stepped aside I would have killed you and let her live!

Balaam said, I am in the wrong! I didn't know that You were standing in the road to bar my way. If I am going wrong in Your sight, I will turn back.

But the angel said, Go with these men, but say only what I tell you to say!

And so Balaam went with the princes of Balak.

When Balak heard that Balaam was on his way, he came out to meet him and said, Why didn't you come the first time I sent for you? You think I am not able to reward you honorably?

Balaam said, Well, now I have come, but I can say only what the Lord puts in my mouth.

In the morning Balak took Balaam to the top of Bamoth-baal where he could look out and see some part of the people of Israel.

Balaam said to Balak, Build me seven altars and prepare me seven bulls and seven rams. Balak did what Balaam said, and on each altar Balak and Balaam offered one bull and one ram.

And Balaam said to Balak, Stand here by your burnt offering. I will walk. Maybe the Lord will meet with me. Whatever He shows me I will tell you.

And he went off and climbed a barren hill. And God met Balaam. The Lord said to Balaam, Go back to Balak. I shall tell you what you are to say to him.

Balaam went back to Balak. Balak stood by his burnt offering with the princes of Moab. And Balaam spoke the Lord's words and said, Balak, the king of Moab, summons me from the mountains of the east and says, Come and curse Jacob for me, come and damn Israel. How can I curse those whom God has not cursed? Or damn those whom the Lord has not damned? From the height of this rock I look down, from these hills I see them—a people set apart and not counted as one among the nations. Who can count the dust of Jacob, or number the fourth part of Israel? May my soul die the death of the righteous, and may my end be like their end!

Balak said, What are you doing to me?

I brought you here to curse my enemies and you—you have blessed them!

Balaam answered, Must I not say what the Lord puts in my mouth?

But Balak said, Come with me! We'll go to another place. From there you can see them, but you'll only see one part of them—you can't see them all. Curse them for me from there!

And Balak took Balaam to the top of Mount Pisgah, and built seven altars and on each altar he offered one bull and one ram. Balaam said to Balak, Stand by your burnt offerings. I will walk and may the Lord meet with me.

And the Lord met with Balaam and put words into his mouth and said, Go back to Balak and say what I have told you.

And he came back to Balak. Balak stood by his offerings with all the princes of Moab. And Balak asked Balaam, What did the Lord say?

And Balaam took up the Lord's words and said: Listen to me, Balak! Hear, King of Moab, what I shall say to you: God is not a man and does not take back His words. He does not change His mind like a mortal man. Should God speak and not act, talk and not do as He says? Know that I have blessed where the Lord has blessed, and I cannot take it back. No harm will come to Jacob, and no misfortune to Israel. The Lord their God is with them. Sorcery or divination cannot hurt them. The time will come when the Lord works His will for Jacob and for Israel. Yes, like a lion this people shall rise up, like a young lion it will rouse itself nor lie down to rest until it has devoured its prey and drunk the blood of its kill.

Balak said to Balaam, Then don't curse them with your curse, only don't bless them with your blessing!

Balaam answered Balak and said, Didn't I tell you I must do whatever the Lord says?

Balak said to Balaam, Come with me! I'll take you to another place. Maybe God will let you curse them for me over there. And Balak took Balaam to the top of Mount Peor, that overlooks the wasteland.

Balaam said to Balak, Build me seven altars here, and prepare me seven bulls and seven rams.

Balak did as Balaam had said and offered one bull and one ram on each altar.

But Balaam saw the Lord was pleased to bless Israel. This time he used no sorcery as he had done before. He turned his face toward the wilderness and Balaam looked and he saw Israel encamped tribe by tribe, and the Spirit of God came upon him and he said: This is the oracle of Balaam whose eyes have been opened, whose ears hear the word of God, who sees a vision of the Almighty and falls upon his knees with opened eyes! How beautiful are your tents, O Jacob, and your dwellings, O Israel! How your valleys wind like gardens on a riverbank, like aloes which the Lord has planted, like cedars beside the waters. Water will flow out of their branches and their roots will have abundant water. Their king will be greater than Agag, their kingdom will be exalted. They will devour their enemy, they will shatter their bones. They will pierce them through with arrows. Like a lion they lie low, they crouch like a young

lion. Who shall dare to rouse them? Blessed are those who bless you and those who curse you shall be accursed!

Balak was very angry with Balaam and he struck his hands together and said, I sent for you to curse my enemies and you have blessed them! These three times you have blessed them! Get away from here! Go home! I said I would reward you with honors, but the Lord has prevented it.

Balaam said, Didn't I tell the messengers you sent for me, If Balak gives me his house full of silver and gold I cannot go against the word of God, either for good or for ill, by my own choosing. What the Lord says, is what I must say. Now I go back to my people, but come! I will tell you what this people will do to your people in days to come! What I see is not yet; I perceive but not soon, that there will rise a star out of Jacob, a scepter out of Israel. It will crush the foreheads of Moab, and the skulls of the sons of Seth. Edom will be conquered, Seir a possession of its enemies. Israel will triumph. A ruler will rise out of Jacob, who will destroy the remnant of your cities!

And Balaam rose and returned home, and Balak also went on his way.

≈ ≈ ≈

AND THE LORD SAID TO MOSES, The time is coming when you must die. Call Joshua and go into the Tent of the Congregation and I shall instruct him.

And they went, Moses and Joshua, and

presented themselves in the tent, and the Lord appeared in a pillar of cloud and the cloud stood over the door of the tent, and the Lord spoke with Moses and said, When you lie in the grave with your fathers, this people will rise up and whore after alien gods in the land which they will enter soon. They will reject Me and break My covenant, which I have made with them. The day will come when My anger shall rage against them. I shall abandon them and hide My face from them and they will be as fodder for the nations. After many evils and troubles have befallen them they will say, Is it because our God is not here with us, in our midst, that these evils fall upon us? On that day I will hide My face and keep it hidden. Write down this song and teach it to the children of Israel and put it in their mouths, and it will be My witness against them. Yes, I shall bring them into the promised land flowing with milk and honey. They will eat and be satisfied and grow fat and turn to other gods and reject Me. I know what they think and what they plot even now, before I have brought them into the promised land.

And the Lord instructed Joshua and said, Be strong and steadfast. It is you who will lead the children of Israel into the promised land. And I, even I, shall be there with you.

And the Lord said, When you cross the Jordan into the land of Canaan, you shall drive out the inhabitants before you and destroy their carved idols and their molten images; you shall demolish their holy places. Take the land and live in it, I have given it into your possession. You shall divide the land by lot among the twelve tribes. Give the larger tribes a larger portion and the smaller tribes a smaller portion. Whatever falls to them by lot shall be their inheritance. But if you do not drive the inhabitants out, the ones you leave alive will become thorns in your eyes and barbs in your sides. They will trouble you in the land on which you will settle. And I will do unto you the things that I had planned to do to them.

And on that day the Lord said to Moses, Go up into the hills of Moab, onto Mount Nebo, and look out over the land of Canaan. I will give it to the children of Israel as their possession. You shall die on that mountain which you will climb and be gathered to your people, like your brother Aaron, who died on the mount of Hor.

And Moses went up from the valley of the Jordan and climbed the top of Mount Pisgah, which lies across from Jericho.

The Lord said, You shall see the promised land from afar, but you shall not enter it, because you did not obey My commandment in the wilderness of Zin, by the waters of Meribah, and did not sanctify Me in the eyes of the children of Israel.

Moses said, Lord, let me go over into that good land beyond the Jordan—to that beautiful mountain!

And the Lord was angry and said, Enough! You shall not go in. And the Lord showed him all that land from Gilead to Dan, and all of Naphtali, and the land of Ephraim and Manasseh, and all of Judah as far as the sea in the west, and the Negev in the south, and the valley

of Jericho, the city of palms, as far as Zoar. And the Lord said, This is the land that I have promised to Abraham, Isaac, and Jacob saying, To your descendants will I give it. Your own eyes have seen it, but you shall not enter.

And Moses, the servant of the Lord, died there, in the land of Moab. He was one hundred and twenty years old, yet his eyes had not failed and his strength had not failed. Israel wept for Moses in the plains of Moab thirty days. And no one to this day knows where he is buried. Never has there risen another prophet in Israel like Moses, with whom the Lord spoke mouth to mouth, like a man speaking to his friend.

The descendants of Cain's son Enoch
invent cities, tools, and the arts.

Noah

Man multiplies and grows wicked;
only Noah is righteous.
God instructs Noah to build the ark.
The flood covers the earth
for forty days and forty nights.
Noah sends out the raven.
He sends out the dove.
The waters withdraw from the earth.
Noah sacrifices to the Lord.
God forbids the shedding of blood.
God makes his covenant with Noah
and sets the rainbow in the sky.

Noah plants the first vineyard
and becomes drunk.
Noah's son Ham exposes his father's nakedness,
but Shem and Japheth cover him
with a cloth.
Noah curses Ham, forefather of the Canaanites,
and blesses his sons Shem and Japheth.

The Tower of Babel

Men plan a tower as high as heaven
but God confuses them
with the multiplicity of language.

The generations,
from Shem to Abraham.

Abraham

God instructs Abraham to leave Haran
and travel to Canaan.
There is famine in Canaan.
Abraham and Sarah sojourn in Egypt.
He begs her to say that she is his sister.
Abraham and his nephew Lot part company.
Lot moves to Sodom.

Isaac

Jacob

Joseph accuses them of spying,
imprisons Simeon,
and sends for his younger brother Benjamin.
The brothers find their money returned
into their sacks.

Famine continues.
The brothers return to Egypt with Benjamin.
Joseph's silver cup
is found in Benjamin's sack.
Judah offers to be Joseph's slave
in Benjamin's stead.
Joseph makes himself known to his brothers.
Joseph is united with his father Jacob,
whom the Lord has named Israel.

Israel blesses Ephraim
before the elder, Manasseh.
Israel dies
and is buried in Canaan.
Joseph dies.

Moses

A new Pharaoh has enslaved
the children of Israel.
He orders Hebrew boys killed at birth.
The midwives Shiphrah and Puah disobey.
Pharaoh's daughter finds the baby Moses
in the rushes
and raises him as her son
in Pharaoh's court.

Moses kills an Egyptian
who is beating a Hebrew,
and flees to Midian.
He sees the daughters of the priest Jethro
at the well.
He marries Zipporah.

Moses sees the Lord in the burning bush.
The Lord commissions Moses
to bring the children of Israel out of Egypt
and lead them to the promised land of Canaan.

The hail stops
and Pharaoh's heart is hardened.

The Lord threatens a plague of locusts.
Pharaoh's court is afraid.
Pharaoh says the Hebrew men may go
if they will leave the women and the children.
Moses says no
and is thrown out of court.
The Lord sends a plague of locusts.
Pharaoh says that he will let the people go
but when the locusts leave
his heart hardens.
He does not let the people go.

The Lord sends a plague of darkness.
Only in Goshen there is light.
Pharaoh says that he will let the people go
if they leave their flocks behind them.
But Moses will not leave a single hoof.

The Lord instructs the children of Israel
to borrow their Egyptian neighbors' gold and silver.
The Lord instructs the children of Israel
to prepare for the Passover.
The Lord strikes down every Egyptian firstborn
but passes over
the houses of the children of Israel.
Now Pharaoh hurries them out of Egypt
and asks for the Lord's blessing.

Moses leads the children of Israel into the wilderness.
The Lord goes before them
as a cloud by day
and a pillar of fire by night.
Pharaoh's army pursues the children of Israel.
Moses divides the waters
and Israel crosses the Red Sea.
The waters return and drown the armies of Egypt.

Moses sings a song of triumph.
Miriam sings her song.

He burns the calf
and hears Aaron's excuses.
Moses instructs the Levite volunteers
to slaughter three thousand of their kin.
Moses returns to the mountain
to beg the Lord's forgiveness.

Moses pitches the Tent of the Congregation
and the Lord speaks with Moses face to face.
The Lord hides Moses in a cleft of the rock
and allows him to see His back.
The Lord makes known to Moses
the list of His attributes.

Moses carves the second tablets
and copies God's commandments.

The skin of Moses' face shines
and he veils himself.

The Lord instructs Moses
to teach Aaron the blessing.

When the cloud covers the Tent,
the children of Israel make camp.
When the cloud lifts,
they continue on their journey.

The rabble demand meat.
Moses begs God to relieve him of the burden
of this grumbling and rebellious people.
The Lord sends His quail to feed them
and His plague to punish them.

Aaron and Miriam rebel against Moses.
God makes Miriam a leper.
Aaron pleads for her with Moses
and Moses pleads with God.

Moses sends twelve spies
into the land of Canaan.
Ten of the spies spread fearful rumors.
The people conspire to choose new leaders
to take them back to Egypt.
The Lord is angry.

He offers to make a new nation out of Moses.
Moses intercedes for Israel.
The Lord curses the children of Israel
and condemns them to wander the wilderness
for forty years.
The repentant people rush into battle
and are routed.

The Lord will not let Balaam go.
When Balak sends a second mission
the Lord lets Balaam go.
Balaam's ass sees the angel in his path,
stops, and gets beaten.
Balak prepares seven altars on Mount Bamoth
to make Balaam curse Israel,
but Balaam blesses Israel.
Balak prepares seven altars on Mount Pisgah,
but Balaam blesses Israel from Mount Pisgah.
Balak tries Mount Peor.
Balaam blesses Israel from Mount Peor.
Balak sends Balaam home with no reward.
Balaam foretells Israel triumphant.

LORE SEGAL has written three novels, *Other People's Houses*, *Lucinella*, and *Her First American*, for which she won an Award in Literature from the American Academy and Institute of Arts and Letters. Among her children's books are *Tell Me a Mitzi*, *Tell Me a Trudy*, and *The Story of Mrs. Lovewright and Purrless Her Cat*. Her work as a translator includes *Gallow Songs* with W. D. Snodgrass and *The Juniper Tree and Other Tales from Grimm* with Randall Jarrell and illustrations by Maurice Sendak. Mrs. Segal lives in New York and teaches at the University of Illinois at Chicago.

∝ ∝ ∝

LEONARD BASKIN has long been a leading figure in the graphics world, with powerfully illustrated editions of the *Iliad*, Dante, and the Haggadah. His recent work includes the drawings for *Flowers and Insects* by Ted Hughes; *The Raptors*, a portfolio of Baskin birds; and several books for children, among them *A Book of Dragons*, written with his son Hosie, and *Leonard Baskin's Miniature Natural History*, which was a *New York Times* Best Illustrated Book of the Year. He is a Caldecott Honor winner, recipient of the National Institute for Arts and Letters' Medal for Graphic Arts, and the American Institute of Graphic Arts' Special Medal of Merit. He lives with his family in Leeds, Massachusetts.